OFFICIAL
BAR & PARTY GUIDE

EDIE HILTON'S

OFFICIAL BAR & PARTY GUIDE

An Original Holloway House Edition

HOLLOWAY HOUSE PUBLISHING CO.
LOS ANGELES, CALIFORNIA

International Standard Book Number 0-87067-486-2

PUBLISHED BY

Holloway House Publishing Company
8060 Melrose Avenue
Los Angeles, California 90046

Printed in the United States of America

CONTENTS

1. THE GUEST LIST

How often have you heard some host or hostess proudly proclaim: "The party was a huge success—we had over two hundred people there!"

What these poor misguided souls don't seem to realize is that they didn't have a party at all. They merely went through an expensive rain dance, similar to conducting a cattle call. Bluntly put, simply luring every pig in town to the slop trough does not turn the event into a festive occasion. Successful elections are insured by a massive turnout of voters. The success of home entertaining is not similarly assured by a massive outpouring of conglomerate humanity.

This popular misconception of social success was probably largely engendered by Hollywood. Who can ever forget the huge cocktail party sequences in which the men all wore black ties and the women slinky low-cut satin gowns? The wall-to-wall party scenes from movies like *Breakfast at*

Tiffany's and *The Great Gatsby* are classic examples of the American Scene that are part of a way of life that is dead and gone.

The day of the "big bash" is a relic of the inglorious past in our national heritage. It has joined vaudeville, the debutante cotillion and the biplane in the archives of our history.

As rapid advances in our methods of transportation and communication have shrunken our world, our social horizons have expanded to a degree that would have been utterly inconceivable to the Emily Posts and Amy Vanderbilts of that bygone era of social graces. Social life has transcended the limits of the once almighty "Four Hundred" and the haughtily aloof pages of the *Social Register*. Our intimate interpersonal contacts with our fellow human beings have become manifoldly more multi-faceted. Most active Americans today find themselves participating in widely divergent areas of subcultures whose aims and interests are often irreconcilable. Any attempt, no matter how well-intended, to bring all of them together under one roof, at one time, could lead only to utter and complete disaster.

It wasn't very many years ago that it was considered the smart and "in" thing for a socially active individual or family to give one huge party a year by means of which they could, with one fell swoop, dispose of an entire year of social obligations. Any attempt to follow this pattern today is destined to be tantamount to social suicide.

It isn't that large parties, per se, are passe in the field of social entertainment. Many still persist and flourish. But when they do it is only because all of the guests, no matter what their numbers, have a basic common denominator. They all attended the same college or university, they are all ardent backers of the same political candidate, they are all active members of the same profession, or something of that sort.

The guest list is the key to the ultimate success or failure of any social gathering. If there is a single secret word which can be ascribed to insuring success, that word is "compatibility."

When people come to a party . . . they drink. If they have widely divergent deep-seated convictions, and someone disagrees with these sacred cow precepts when they are drinking . . . they argue violently. It is of just such stuff that barroom brawls are made. Don't risk turning your home into an arena for any such choosing-up of sides and resultant violent confrontations.

The first thing to bear in mind is that you are not using your planned party as a means of impressing any and all of your guests with the widespread drawing power of your social appeal. You'll be infinitely better off by giving a number of small parties for which you have carefully analyzed and categorized those on your guest list than in attempting to give one big bash that may end in a big blowup.

Bring together in your home, on any one occasion, only those guests whom you believe to be socially compatible. The keynote for success in a party is that your guests enjoy not just themselves, but one another. They want to make friends that they feel are "their kind of people." You want to bring them into contact with people whom they will like and want to get to know better. When your guests exchange names and phone numbers and make plans to see each other for lunch or dinner, this is an ultimate compliment to your good taste. Your stock will go up in their books because they'll consider you as being a member of the "in group" among their kind of people.

By Edie Hilton

At an oversized party the guests are like delegates at a convention. They shake hands and smile at a great many people but seldom have a chance to enter into meaningful conversation with them or get the feeling that they know any of them any better at the end of the evening.

The smaller, intimate party is the socially "in" thing these days. This generally ranges from three or four couples with much in common up to perhaps twenty or thirty people with some general area of common interest. These are the parties that most guests find most enjoyable and most memorable. From a strictly selfish viewpoint, such guests are far more likely to reciprocate your hospitality by inviting you to similar get-togethers in their homes than are the participants in a cocktail mob scene, many of whom may well think that you are simply trying to outdo whatever reciprocal efforts they might make.

Every party should have an underlying theme or purpose to which each and every guest can readily relate. You could scarcely expect a retired millionaire to relate to the mood of celebration of a "Thank God It's Friday" party that would have meaning only for members of the working classes. By the same token you wouldn't invite a black friend or the local Catholic priest to a party honoring the Grand Wizard of the Ku Klux Klan. Use similar judgment in checking your guest list for every party you plan to host, and you'll have taken the first giant step toward the success of the occasion.

The guests at a party should be carefully selected to complement and augment one another. Your good judgment in establishing such a compatible guest list will go infinitely further to impress than any consideration such as the sheer weight of numbers.

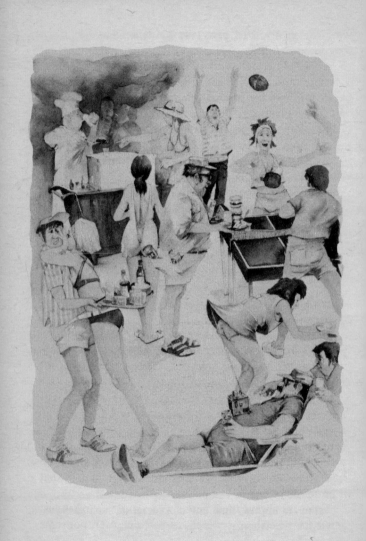

2. HOW LONG SHOULD THE BASH LAST?

How long a successful party should last is as frequently a misunderstood consideration as how many guests one should invite to it.

We have all had the experience receiving an invitation clearly stating: *Cocktails: five to seven p.m.* In spite of this intended limitation on drinking hours stipulated by the host and hostess, we've seen the last of the guests being poured into their automobiles long after midnight. Sometimes this is because there are certain types of guests who aren't about to leave until the free well of booze runs dry. Other times it is because the host and hostess are having such a fun time that they virtually won't let their guests leave. On such occasions we're often moved to ask: "What is protocol?"

There are always those guests who arrive late, often just about the time the party is supposed to be over. For some reason many of these people feel that they are, in spite of their tardiness, entitled to a full two hours of free booze. Because they remain long after the expiration period of their invitation, they inspire the "Freddy the Freeloader" types to hang in there and swill up the free spirits. If the host and hostess get a little smashed themselves, they may well wind up feeding breakfast to a number of their two-hour cocktail time guests!

Over an extended period of time in any given social group, the people who emerge as the most popular and sought-after guests are those who arrive on time—and leave on time.

Party protocol is based upon punctuality. You would be well-advised to observe this rule as a host or hostess as religiously as you would as a guest.

When you invite guests to join you for drinks from five to seven and they arrive at six-forty-five, you are not being an inconsiderate or impolite host to feed them one drink and shoo them out by explaining that you have a dinner engagement at seven-thirty. The next time you invite them they'll jolly well arrive on time!

In spite of these general considerations of plain common-sense etiquette and good manners, the overall question of just how long a party should last is, in the final analysis, based upon just how long the host, hostess and guests are enjoying it and themselves. A party may be planned to last five hours (about normal), but if the guests are bored after an hour and a half, that's when they should leave. If the host and hostess are bored or annoyed with their guests after two hours, that's when they should close the bar and call the gala festivities to an abrupt halt. It's a two-way street; don't be afraid to enforce traffic regulations on it.

The time-span element of a party is no measure of its success. Better to give a fast, fun one than a long-drawn-out dull one.

Ways In Which To Speed the Parting Guest:

There is an old saying which proclaims: "Never give a person who's had too much to drink a cup of coffee. If you do, you'll wind up with a wide-awake drunk on your hands—and there's nothing worse!"

When the bulk of the guests have left and you're stuck with a few stragglers—as one always is—simply put the booze away, toss out the remaining ice cubes and close down the bar. Then begin to go around and turn out the lights, check to see that the doors and windows are locked, and put out the cat for the night. If they still don't get the hint, ask if they're in shape to drive home or if they want you to call them a cab.

A good final line is a blunt: "We have no guest room because we *detest* guests, but you're perfectly welcome to sleep in the geranium beds out front."

When all else has failed, simply grasp your guest beneath the armpits, drag to front door, open door and heave-ho!

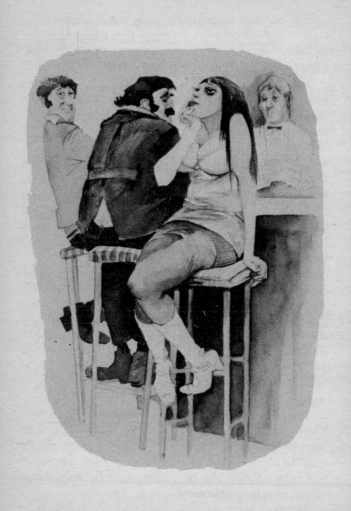

3. SPECIAL OCCASIONS

Everybody and his brother gives birthday parties, engagement parties, graduation parties, wedding anniversary parties and bon voyage or going away parties. Many socially active people actually come to dread invitations to these "command appearance" affairs. From a somewhat antisocial but highly practical viewpoint, they often are moved to feel that the virtually mandatory gift they must bring costs more than the free booze and grub is worth.

Everybody gives parties for Valentine's Day, Halloween, Fourth of July, St. Patrick's Day and you name it. Such days on the calendar constitute the social highlights of the year. Often months go by between them with no action on the social scene. So why not create a special occasion out of no occasion for a welcome change of party pace?

Just for openers, how about a Groundhog Day party, or

an intimate get-together to celebrate the sixth anniversary of Joan's divorce from Bill, Helen's abortion or Sally's miscarriage? Several active fan clubs in Hollywood give annual memorial birthday parties for their long-gone movie idols like Gary Cooper, Humphrey Bogart and W.C. Fields. Film posters and memorabilia serve as special occasion party decor. There's always a big birthday cake and, at one point during the evening, this bunch of congenial drunks gather around the table with the unoccupied chair for the guest of honor and sing "Happy Birthday to You." Corny, but different.

Possibilities are limitless, and you can let your imagination run rampant. How about a party to celebrate getting fired from that lousy job and not having to face that bastard of a boss any more? The kinkier the excuse, the better. Perhaps the one that tops them all is the "We're giving a party to celebrate the fact that we couldn't think of any other excuse" party.

A popular gimmick of the early Thirties was the Depression party. Nobody in those dreary days had enough money to throw a party so it became a joint effort among the guests. The guys all brought booze and the gals all brought food. The idea enjoyed a revival during World War II in the B.Y.O.B. (Bring Your Own Bottle) parties given by low-income military families.

One recent variety of the "no excuse for a party" party is the "We Don't Have a Damn Thing To Do, So Why Don't You Come Over And Help Us Do It" party.

The total informality and unplanned aspects of social get-togethers of this type is the basis of their appeal. Next time you feel bored and socially jaded, why not give such an idea a try?

4. INVITATIONS AND ACCEPTANCES

One of the most difficult things for the average inexperienced party giver to do is to issue invitations. Should they be issued verbally? If so, is it better to phone someone at home or to invite him in person when you see him? Or is it considered more proper to send a written invitation to each guest? How do you know who'll show up and who won't? Is all this old R.S.V.P. jazz still necessary?

Invitations:

Invitations to any party from the simplest cocktail gathering to a formal sit-down dinner party should *always* be in writing and sent by mail.

Don't think you're being more proper to handwrite a little note or letter of invitation. These can too easily get mixed in with other mail or discarded. When an invited guest forgets the date of a party it's easier not to come than

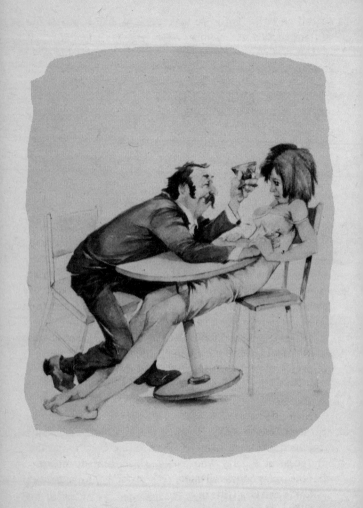

to call and ask. To do so makes it look like it wasn't important enough to remember or enter on his calendar.

Use one of the printed invitation forms available at all greeting card counters. Pick one that is distinctive enough in appearance to stand out among other mail. There's so much fancy-looking junk mail littering our letterboxes today that many a party invitation is thrown out because it doesn't *look* like an invitation.

The ideal card will clearly state that it is an invitation and announce what kind of a party it is, when and where. Choose one that announces in big, bold type:

"YOU are INVITED to a COCKTAIL PARTY!"

Such cards provide spaces for the date and time, usually listed as From: Till:_____ . The better type guests will make it a point to leave on or before the appointed time you've filled in at Till:_____. If you want the party to continue as long as everybody is having a good time, simply put a question mark in the Till:__?__ spot. Another way to handle this situation is to do it this way: Till: we run outta' booze and food!

If the party is for some special occasion this should be so stated on the invitation:

"Surprise Party for Madge's Birthday."

"Farewell Get-Together for Ethel and Harry."

"To celebrate Frank's promotion."

. . . or whatever.

If the occasion calls for a gift, this should also be carefully mentioned. Nothing is more embarrassing than to be the only guest at a party who didn't bring a present or know what the occasion was all about. It's perfectly proper to say:

"Cards and Gag Gifts in order."

"Gifts under $5.00 welcome."

"Harriet taking up collection for special present."

or . . .

"Just bring yourselves and a husky thirst!"

These are informal times, and a lot of things that would have been social taboos a few years back are now considered quite normal and proper. Especially in the case of young working people, it is perfectly proper and socially acceptable to include such a line as:

"B.Y.O.B."

"Bring whatever you plan to drink more of than I have on hand."

or . . .

"Contributions to bar or buffet gratefully accepted."

Don't think that this marks you as a cheapie or a square. It doesn't at all.

The old R.S.V.P. (*repondez s'il vous plait*) has all but disappeared from informal invitations. When used for more formal affairs such as sit-down dinners, wedding receptions and the like, it should include a small return card and envelope so the host or hostess will know if he can count on your appearance. If a reply is asked for it should, by all means, be dispatched promptly. Many such parties are catered, and the person giving the party must give a guarantee to the caterer well ahead of time. If you and your wife or date are expected but don't show up, the host and hostess can be out twenty to fifty bucks. That's a pretty shabby way to thank them for the kindness of inviting you.

For more informal parties it is proper and practical to say:

"Will expect you unless I hear to the contrary."

"Let us know only if you can't make it."

or . . .

"Show up or call with your excuse!"

The invitation should always include the phone number of the person giving the party.

If an invited guest has never been to your home before and it's hard to find or on a little-known street, give instructions or a simple map.

In cases where you frequently see guests that you've invited at work or other activities and, after mailing an invitation to them, they make no mention of receiving it, it's perfectly all right to ask:

"You're coming to my party, aren't you?"

or . . .

"Did you get my invitation for cocktails on June 4th?"

With the postal service becoming more irregular and undependable, there is always a chance that their invitation might have gone astray in the mails. It's surely less embarrassing for you to have to ask them to acknowledge the invitation than for them to hear about the party from others and think they were purposely excluded.

Acceptances:

The best thing to do, as soon as you receive an invitation, is to check your calendar, make sure you are, or are not, available on the specified date, then phone the person to acknowledge receipt of the invitation, thank them for having included you and then accept with pleasure or give your regrets that you'll be unable to attend. Once this is done, enter the date on your calendar and put the invitation in a prominent place as a reminder.

The Negative Invitation:

Few people have ever given a party that didn't find themselves stuck with a few "duty invitation" guests. It seems to be one of Murphy's Laws that "the people you hope can't make it, always can."

The problem of inviting an unwanted guest in such a way that you can expect the invitation to be turned down rather than accepted but with no hurt feelings is one of the most provocative ones in the whole realm of home entertaining.

Here's a pretty safe way of resolving this dilemma. Go ahead and send the unwanted guest an invitation at the same time you mail out the ones to guests you really want. Then, before the invitation has a chance to reach them by mail, phone them. Tell them about the invitation that they will be receiving and how much you *were* looking forward to seeing them, *but*—you just found out that you were being stuck with two of the biggest bores ever to "wet blanket" an otherwise happy occasion. You can't call the party off, much as you'd like to, and you feel guilty at subjecting people to what promises to be the dullest evening on record. You are, *however,* calling a few of your closest and dearest friends to warn them away from what is sure to be a disaster zone. You're already making plans for a *real fun* party as soon as you get rid of Mr. and Mrs. Dull and will be phoning them about it soon.

If you handle it right, the unwanted guest will love rather than hate you for it. If they have any tact at all, they'll explain that they couldn't have made it anyway due to a previous social commitment. They'll figure that if you didn't want them to come you simply wouldn't have sent them an invitation. Since you did, they were wanted. Even more so in that you were considerate enough to let them in on a little inside "warning" that the others weren't sharing.

You can vary this approach to suit the situation and personality of those involved. An adaptation of the same technique will smooth the slightly ruffled feathers or hurt feelings of those who ask:

"How come you didn't invite me to your party next Saturday?"

A Good and Welcome Guest:

At first this may seem somewhat out of place in a book devoted to how to give a party and be a host or hostess. It is included simply because experienced party givers have learned that it is virtually impossible to learn the art of being a gracious host or hostess until one has developed the knack of being a good guest.

Never arrive empty-handed. Even if you have phoned to ask, "Can I bring anything?" and been told "No," bring it anyway. If it's a cocktail party, a gift-wrapped bottle for the bar is always appreciated. It doesn't have to be the most expensive Scotch, either. A medium grade of vodka will do nicely. It's seldom that your host or hostess will unwrap it immediately. When you arrive simply display your contribution and say: "Where's the bar, I'll put this small offering on the sacrificial altar of Bachus." You don't have to go all out. Later, they won't know who brought what anyway.

If it's a dinner party, a bottle of wine, nicely gift-wrapped, will serve the purpose admirably. Here again, take a middle-of-the-road approach. If you bring something better than they'll be serving with dinner, this could embarrass them and might even be taken as a put-down.

Flowers should never be brought to the party, but should be delivered earlier, by the florist, with a little "Thanks for Your Hospitality" card bearing your name. When guests are arriving is no time for a host or hostess to be stuck in the kitchen finding a vase and putting flowers in water.

Saying "Thank You":

In the more elegant era of a generation or so ago the "bread-and-butter" note or phone call a day or two after a party was considered mandatory if you ever wanted to be invited back again.

In recent years all too many people have come to feel that simply saying, "Good night and thank you. I had a lovely time," sufficiently discharges their social obligation as an expression of appreciation.

Parties are a bother and an expense. The host or hostess who gives one has devoted a great deal of time and effort to insure that the guests have a pleasant few hours within their home. Surely this entitles them to more than simply a cursory, "G'night, T'was fun," at the end of the evening.

The person who takes the time and trouble to send a little "Thank you for the wonderful time" note or to telephone and say how much he enjoyed himself and how grateful he is to have been included will rank high on the guest list for the future parties.

Reciprocal Invitations:

If you've been invited to dinner and you phone to say "Thank you again," don't feel that you have to extend a return invitation immediately. Actually, this is somewhat in poor taste. It appears that you're trying to even the score and clean the slate by disposing of a social obligation as expediently as possible. Better to let a few weeks go by, then make plans and extend your invitation, which should preferably include other people who weren't at the party you attended.

5. THE BARTENDER'S BASIC TRAINING

According to an old proverb, "There are tricks to every trade."

There are few trades as tricky as that of the bartender. Recognizing this fact, every state has passed very strict laws to regulate and control the preparation of alcoholic beverages for public sale. Each state, under varying titles, has its own version of California's Alcoholic Beverage Control Board, more commonly known as the ABC. Inspectors from this agency made periodic scheduled and unscheduled inspections looking for violations. They also maintain large staffs of plainclothes officers who frequent bars, posing as customers. If they have reason to suspect any violations they are prepared to make tests and chemical analysis of drinks served. Proven violations can result in suspension of the state license to sell alcoholic drinks for up to six months. Repeated violations can result in cancellation of the license.

Since a liquor license is (depending upon the state) worth between ten and twenty-five thousand dollars most bar and restaurant owners are very strict to see that the letter of the law is observed by their employees.

Although such regulatory acts need be of no direct concern to the home bartender, there is much to be learned from a brief review of some of the things that they cover.

1. Misrepresentation by Label:

Basically this refers to the common practice among the "clip joint" nightclubs of World War II days of filling empty bottles of an expensive brand with a cheaper and inferior brand. It has been extended in most areas to simply state that it is illegal to pour any alcoholic beverage into a labeled bottle. You can only pour it *out*, not *in*. This explains why you'll often see two half-empty bottles of the same brand behind a bar. Even though the contents are identical, it would be illegal to use a funnel and pour one half-empty into the other.

Call brands are generally more expensive than non-call brands which come from lesser-known or less-expensive labels of booze "in the well" (under the counter, rather than on open display on the back bar).

If you order a "bourbon and soda" you'll get whatever brand is "in the well." If you order Jack Daniels and soda and the bartender pours the well brand, he's in deep Bandini if an ABC spotter sees him do it.

2. Hiding the Well:

The customer has the right to know what the well brand is that he is being served. Many bars post a sign stating the brands of Scotch, bourbon, vodka and gin that they use in their wells. If asked, the bartender cannot simply name the brand but is legally required to remove the bottle from the well and display the label.

3. Uncapped Bottles:

A bottle cannot be left open so that dust might be allowed to settle on the surface of its contents. Because it would be impractical for a busy bartender to uncork and recork a bottle or screw a cap on and off it each time he poured a drink, most bars provide their open stock bottles with pourer spouts. These are either plastic or metal and feature a little built-in trap door to keep them dust-tight between pourings.

4. Breakage of Empties:

Since it is illegal for even the original distiller to refill an empty bottle, most states require that the empties be broken so as to make re-use impossible. Most bar owners keep close track of this so-called "breakage" as a means of determining how much money should be in the register for a given shift.

5. Sterilization of Glasses:

This is highly controlled. Each glass must be washed with a brush in a hot disinfectant-laden water and rinsed three times. Purity of ice cubes is also checked.

There are an infinite number of other regulatory laws such as not serving minors or intoxicated patrons and the like. In spite of these and the concerted efforts of ABC personnel and bar owners to enforce them rigidly, a number of unprincipled bartenders will use a variety of dodges to cheat and steal from both their employers and their customers. A few of these will be of interest to you, not just as a bar patron, but because they will indicate a few of the tricks you can use, quite legally, to minimize expenses in both stocking and dispensing from your own home bar.

1. Cheating the Almighty P.C.:

Every bar owner establishes and holds his bartenders highly responsible for maintaining that establishment's individual "P.C." This is the means by which the owner or manager controls his cost and profit ratios.

There is a general misconception that "P.C." means "percentage." Actually the letters stand for "pouring count" by means of which they know exactly how many drinks should be sold for each bottle purchased. You'll soon see how this works for you in your home bar.

Many bartenders drink on the job. This soon shows up on their pouring count. Since they're stealing it anyway, they'll usually help themselves to the best. Others have girl friends or buddies to whom they slip drinks. They have to make up the difference somewhere. Some will charge slightly loaded customers for more drinks than they actually had, hoping to put the difference in the till that way. Others will substitute cheap well whiskey for the good stuff customers' order that they've already drunk themselves.

Far and away the most popular methods are to load the tabs of customers with charge accounts, figuring they won't remember how many drinks they had, or bought for others, when they get their bill weeks later, and the most prevalent practice of all:

2. Short Pouring or "Highballing 5/8ths":

When the bartender can't make up for his, and his friends', personal consumption and still maintain his P.C., he will fill in the difference by short-pouring transient customers or regulars who've had so much already they won't know the difference. Instead of the usual ounce and a quarter he will "highball five-eighths of an ounce." For each two such drinks he serves he is making up for one of his.

3. Short-Changing:

This is a popular practice by means of which the bartender who is still short on his P.C. can put the couple of bucks he's short into the register and the balance in his pocket or tip jar. It's generally pulled on customers who are sufficiently in their cups not to notice whether they gave him a ten or a twenty.

The surest way to avoid being victimized by this old ruse is to ask: "How much do I owe you?" rather than just shoving a bill across the bar. Once he tells you, announce the denomination of the bill you give him, by saying: "Out of twenty." Not only will he realize that you're aware of how much you gave him but, if he tries to pull any tricks, there is a good chance that other customers will have overheard you and gang up on him.

Adapting This to Your Home Bar:

You are, of course, not subject to any stringent laws in your own home. If you have two half-empties of the same or even different brands, there's nothing in the world to stop you from using a funnel and consolidating them into one to avoid overcrowding.

The great "Brand Name Hoax" is nowhere more prevalent than in the liquor industry. The high-priced brands are generally so because of the large percentage of the sales price that goes into advertising. Even so, don't be misled by the "confidential inside dope" offered by discount houses and chain drug stores that would tell you: "This is the same as Cutty Sark at half the price." No confirmed Cutty Sark drinker would be fooled by it for a moment. There are, to be sure, certain private label brands that are the same as advertised brands. You'll be more likely to find these at the country club, exclusive private clubs and well-known restaurants and hotels. Some clubs make these private label brands available to their members in case lots. Generally they are about twenty percent cheaper than their advertised counterparts and you won't have to hide the labels.

Smart Shopping for Liquor:

In buying booze for home consumption it is both possible and practical to be frugal without being chintzy. Here are a few simple suggestions that can add up to substantial savings in your party and entertainment budget:

1. Always buy liquor in "case lots." A case consists of twelve bottles but this doesn't mean that you have to take a dozen of each item you'll need. Most liquor stores will be happy to sell you a "split case" which can consist of two or three bottles each of Scotch, bourbon, gin and vodka and still give you the ten percent discount on the total. If your dealer won't, find one who will.

2. Avoid unknown or "bargain" brands. Liquor, like anything else, is generally worth just what you pay for it.

3. Don't pose as an authority on spirits and wines. The liquor store man has spent a lifetime acquiring genuine knowledge of the subject. Seek his advice. Tell him you want good quality without unnecessarily overpaying for it.

He'll want to make a steady customer of you and will go out of his way to help you become a smart shopper.

4. Divide your requirements into high and medium quality of each type of liquor needed. Here are a few specific suggestions by brand names for various spirits:

Vodka: Avoid imported vodka. Chances are your guests won't like it and can't handle it. It's more like a liqueur meant to be drunk straight. It is extremely potent. In the mixed vodka drinks popular with Americans, it imparts a strange, almost brackish, taste that most people can't appreciate. You'll be buying something terribly expensive and accused of serving cheap rotgut.

Originally there were two top brands of American vodka, Smirnoff and Wolfschmidt. Both were the same quality and the same price. Because of Smirnoff's larger distribution facilities, they began to dominate the quality vodka market. Wolfschmidt countered this by dropping their price over $2.00 a fifth with no lowering in quality. Today, the smart buyers call for it. Even so, some people still demand Smirnoff because of its reputed snob appeal. Buy one bottle of Smirnoff and back it up with two of Wolfschmidt. Serve the Smirnoff only to those who call for it by name. Use the Wolfschmidt *only* for vodka on the rocks, vodka martinis, and vodka and tonic.

Back these up with three bottles of a reasonable, but not the very cheapest, vodka. There are lots of good brands selling between $3.50 and $4.00 a fifth. Use these for Bloody Marys, screwdrivers, vodka and Coke and all similar drinks in which the flavor of the vodka cannot be tasted anyway.

Always buy 80 proof vodka, never 100 proof for home

use.

Scotch: Chivas Regal is the snob appeal Scotch. It costs about $5.00 a fifth more than excellent popular brands. If you are having guests you need to impress, invest in one bottle only. Use this *only* for those who ask for it and drink their Scotch on the rocks, straight, or with just a splash of water. Even so, after the third drink switch them to your back-up brand. Scotch has a tendency to anesthetize the palate to the point that even an expert can't tell the difference after the third drink.

Your best all-around bet in Scotch is Cutty Sark. It is moderately priced and the world's most popular brand of Scotch whiskey. Even though some guests may ask for another brand, they're usually happy to settle for "Cutty." After all, you're not running a full "call brand" type of public bar.

Never buy a cheap Scotch. You simply can't get away with it. Besides, you won't save enough to make it worth the embarrassment when your friends ask: "What's this?"

Bourbon: Buy one bottle of Jack Daniels. It's the bourbon connoisseur's brand. Serve it only to those who ask for it by name and drink it on the rocks, straight, or with a splash of water or soda.

Back this up with three bottles of Jim Beam. It's almost as good and costs about $3.00 less per fifth. Use this for bourbon and soda and bourbon-based cocktails. Never put Jack Daniels in coke or ginger ale, even if someone orders it (unless they're watching you mix it). These sickly-sweet mixes negate the delicate nutlike flavor of this expensive sour mash and it is simply a criminal waste of good whiskey.

Give them the Jim Beam. They'll never be any the wiser.

Never buy a cheap bourbon. The savings may appear attractive but they can have disastrous results. The excessive fusel oil content can cause nausea and produce violent hangovers.

Gin: Your best bet here is to stick to either Gordon's or Gilbey's or one bottle of each. Forget the fancy brands like Bols Holland gin or Bombay gin. You can't be expected to stock everything and you won't get enough calls for it to warrant giving up the space it would take.

Some people like Tangueray gin but you don't have to bother to stock it. You can fake it by mixing half gin and half vodka. Not one person in a hundred can tell that from the original expensive brand in which they've done little more than pre-mix the two at the distillery.

Gin drinkers are a breed apart and you can't pull the wool over their eyes, or taste buds, with an inferior brand. Besides, there's no such thing on the market as a *good* cheap gin!

Brandy: Brandy is something for which few people in this country ever develop an analytical taste. Many try to hide their ignorance of the subject by calling for such snob appeal brands as Courvoisier or Cordon Bleu and occasionally Martel or Hennessey.

Forget it. Stick to Christian Brothers. It is a fine quality, aromatic brandy at a reasonable price. Many brandy buffs prefer it to the infinitely higher-priced imports.

Wines: Wine is increasing in popularity in the United States faster than any other beverage. There are more books

sold on wine than there are bartender's guides. This has given birth to a vast number of self-appointed wine experts. Most of these clowns are as phony as three-dollar bills.

Sherry is the only wine that warrants stocking an expensive brand. There are two and it's a good idea to keep one of each on hand, since they are not readily interchangeable among their devotees. One is Dry Sack and the other Harvey's Bristol Cream sherry. These are extremely popular among older people.

The current crop of California wines is as fine as any in the world. As proof of this, more California wine is exported annually to France and Italy than the total of American imports from their old established vineyards!

As a general rule, steer clear of the sweet wines. Keep a good stock of light, dry, white and red wines. Your best bet is to buy them in case lots. Here again you can split a case into half white and half red and still be entitled to the ten percent case lot discount.

Among the white wines, the most generally popular is dry Chablis. Among the light dry red wines, one with near-universal appeal is Cabernet Sauvignon. Good, inexpensive brands are Almaden and Paul Masson. Vin Rose is a pink dry wine midway between the two. A split case consisting of four bottles of each of these three types is a safe investment.

All wines should be stored lying down (so as to keep the corks moist) until just before use. White wines should be chilled before serving; red wines, not. Once opened, a bottle of white wine should be placed in a bucket of ice between pourings.

Champagne and Sparkling Wines: Champagne parties are

becoming extremely popular, largely because they constitute infinitely less effort on the part of the host-bartender.

There are three basic types of sparkling wines: champagne, sparkling burgundy, and Cold Duck, which is about midway between the other two as a sort of sparkling Vin Rose.

There are many excellent domestic champagnes that are quite reasonably priced. Many champagne lovers claim that among American sparkling wines, the best come from New York State where the climate of the vineyards more closely approaches that of the grape's native France. Among these brands, Taylor's is very good and moderately priced.

Champagne is somewhat like Scotch whiskey in that it very quickly deadens the palate. For an economical champagne party, start with Taylor's for the first three glasses served to each guest and then switch off to an even less expensive California brand. Among these, Andre's and La Domaine are excellent for your purposes.

All sparkling wines must be served in the proper size and shape of glass to taste right. Such glasses are especially designed to make fullest use of the delicate bouquet and bubbles. For large parties, champagne glasses and even fountains from which guests can refill their own can be rented reasonably from party rental agencies.

Mixes: The proper mix is vital to a successful drink. Don't try to skimp on this least expensive but highly important element in stocking your bar. Off-brands should be avoided. Canada Dry and Schweppes are your safest choice. As with liquors, most stores give a ten percent discount when mix is bought in case lots. Because of its low cost, however, they don't like to split cases.

Ice Cubes: Fresh, crystal-clear ice cubes are an essential element of a good drink. There's nothing more frustrating than running out of ice halfway through a party. A good rule of thumb to calculate your requirements is to figure on one pound of cubes per guest. This allows for melting, cubes left in glasses, etc.

Even if your refrigerator-freezer is equipped with an automatic icemaker, you'll be better off to lay in a supply of commercial cubes. Ice which remains too long in a freezer or refrigerator gets stale and brackish by picking up odors from foods stored in with it.

Most major liquor stores have commercial ice machines. If you buy your liquor and mix from them and give them sufficient advance notice, they'll usually provide you with your needs at no charge. Even if you need one hundred pounds, they'll figure that for that much ice you'll need a lot of booze so it behoves them to be generous.

If not, there are commercial ice houses listed in the yellow pages of the phone book where twenty-five and fifty-pound bags of cubes in insulated containers are available at low cost. They'll load them into the trunk of your car for you. If you have to carry them in alone, you'll be well advised to stick to the twenty-five-pound bags. Nothing puts a crimp in a party like the host having a heart attack lugging ice just before it starts!

Large bags of commercial cubes often tend to stick together in clumps. You'd be well-advised to invest in a "cube-cracker" to separate them. This is a metal paddle device mounted on a rather flexible shaft. Most liquor and hardware stores carry them at about a dollar or two. They are sheer magic at separating cubes which have fused together. In an emergency a large stainless steel cooking spoon can be used. Hold it lightly by the handle and slap at the stuck-together cubes with the rounded back of the spoon with rather flexible blows, more like you were using a fly swatter than a hammer.

Controlling the P.C. of Your Home Bar:

Many inexperienced party givers labor under the delusion that they'll use less liquor by somewhat underpouring their guests' drinks. Surprisingly, just the opposite is the case. If you feed everybody weak drinks they'll down them like water and keep popping back for refills. If you give them fairly stiff belts, they'll nurse their drinks and, at the end of the party, you'll actually have used less booze.

Never, but never, use a measuring cup or jigger of any kind. It's the mark of a rank amateur and carries with it the psychological implication that you are rationing them on how much they should consume. Always free-pour and, if in doubt, go a little on the heavy side. If you're making the drinks too stiff for a guest, he or she will not hesitate to tell you so. If you make them too weak, only the most gauche of guests would think of mentioning it.

Without knowing the size glass you'll be using, any advice in ounces would be meaningless. A good rule of thumb is to put the ice cubes in first; two cubes in a rocks or lowball drink, three to four in a highball, depending on how tall the glass is. Now pour in the booze. It should come slightly above the halfway point over the ice cubes. In short, the ice and liquor should half fill the glass. Next add the mix to about the three-quarter mark of the glass. If a guest wants more mix there will be no thought of embarrassment in asking for it. It's much easier to ask a host or hostess for more mix than for more booze!

How To Be A Guest At Your Own Party:

Nothing can make a guest feel more uncomfortable than to watch a host or hostess working like a servant in his or her own home in order to entertain them. Since you're the one who's footing the bill, you ought to have at least as much fun as your freeloading friends.

If you have a small to medium-sized group of intimate friends, it is considered quite socially acceptable to mix each guest the first drink and tell them to help themselves from there on in. It's done in the best of circles. Often a number of the men guests enjoy taking turns serving as bartender. That's perfectly okay, too.

If it's a larger group or perhaps one which includes a number of business acquaintances and others whom you want to spend time with and get to know better, you'd be well-advised to hire a party bartender for the occasion and perhaps a girl to serve hors d'oeuvres and pick up empty glasses, clean the ashtrays, and do all the little odds and ends that are so important and time-consuming. Since you're in this deep, another fifty bucks or so would be a sound investment if it doubled the effectivity of the overall project. Besides, it adds an air of elegance that lends an even more festive air to the event. Your favorite bar or restaurant will know of people who are available for such part-time work and their rates and reliability. Figure that one bartender can handle fifty hard drinking guests.

In this way you can be a guest at your own party and devote your full attention to your guests and not the myriad details of throwing a party. The investment will seem doubly wise when you wake up the next morning with a hangover and perhaps a new-found roommate and find the place neat and tidy instead of an after-party disaster zone.

6. SETTING UP YOUR BAR

There are so many factors to be taken into consideration when setting up a bar that any suggestions made here can be taken as guidelines in their broadest sense. Budget, personal taste, space and many other items must be taken into account before preparing a shopping list. However, the well-stocked bar should contain most, if not all, of the following spirits:

2 bottles straight bourbon
1 bottle blended bourbon
1 bottle rye whiskey
1 bottle Canadian whiskey
2 bottles Scotch
1 bottle Irish whiskey
1 bottle London dry gin (for martinis)
1 bottle domestic gin (for cocktails)

1 bottle dark rum
1 bottle medium rum
1 bottle white rum
2 bottles vodka
1 bottle tequila
1 bottle VSOP Cognac
1 bottle domestic brandy (for cocktails)
1 bottle dry sherry
1 bottle cream sherry
1 bottle port
1 bottle dry vermouth
1 bottle sweet vermouth
Assorted liqueurs (Benedictine, Chartreuse, Curacao, Galliano, Grand Marnier, Creme de Cacao, cherry brandy, etc.)

These are the basics. It looks a formidable list, but one must remember that many of the items will remain intact for a long time and only a small percentage will need replacing. In all this list adds up to thirty-two fifths of liquor, and that shouldn't set you back much more than $250.00. So you've got your booze. Now you need something to mix it with. Here is another checklist:

Fruit juices (orange, grapefruit, sweet and sour, pineapple, lemon, tomato, lime, passion fruit, etc.)
Sodas (club soda, Coca-Cola, 7 Up, carbonated water, ginger ale)
Ice (crushed and cube)
Bitters (Angostura and orange)
Sauces (Worcestershire and Tobasco)
Salt (regular, coarse, and celery salt)

Pepper (finely fresh ground black)
Lemons and limes
Cherries (maraschino and green mint)
Cinnamon sticks
Grenadine
Fresh mint
Olives (small green pitted)
Cocktail onions
Sugar (superfine)
Milk and cream
Coffee
Eggs

Bar Equipment:

Much of the equipment for the bar can be stolen from the kitchen, but there are a few special items which are indespensible for the truly professional touches:

Cocktail shaker (silver may be very chic but it tarnishes, so get a shaker made of stainless steel or chromium plated)
Blender (a professional bar blender with a metal cannister is by far the best, but a regular household blender will do)
Bar spoons (get at least three—they're always getting lost)
Sharp knives (for cutting and peeling fruit)
Cutting board
Corkscrew
Cocktail sticks
Coasters
Swizzle sticks

Cocktail napkins
Ice cube-cracker (or large cooking spoon)

Glasses:

In the recipes listed elsewhere in this publication, several types of glasses are mentioned. It is not essential to have all of them, but the correct glass for each drink does add a touch of class.

Unless you are very well off we recommend that you do not use crystal or hand-blown glass for your home bar. It just gets too expensive when it breaks—and it will get broken. Don't serve your drinks in plastic cups, but don't spend five bucks a glass either. Get good, clear machine-blown glassware, and make sure you buy a style of glassware that can be easily replaced, so you don't end up with a bunch of mismatched glasses. The types of glasses you'll need for an all-round bar are:

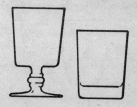

The old-fashioned or on-the-rocks glass. Just about any kind of mixed drink can be served in this glass, and you'll find you need more of them than any other kind.

The cocktail glass, which holds from 4½ to 6 ounces.

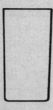

This tall straight glass is used for highballs, collins and coolers, and comes from 8 to 12 ounces in size.

The standard 1½ ounce (1 jigger) shot glass used mainly for measuring, but also for serving straight shots.

This is the sour glass, also called a Delmonico, and is

available in from 4½ to 7 ounce sizes.

The conventional (American) champagne glass is better used for champagne cocktails.

Something like the all-purpose wine glass, this is the best type of glass to serve champagne in, since it holds the bubbles and the wine stays sparkling longer.

Just about any kind of large glass can be used to serve beer, but the Pilsner is the best, as it is specially designed to keep the beer cold and fizzing.

The liqueur, cordial or pony glass. It holds 1 ounce.

The brandy snifter, holding from 2 to 8 ounces. The 8

ounce glass is best since it allows the drinker to swirl the
drink around, releasing the full aroma of the brandy.

The modern all-purpose wine glass. It must be clear (un-
tinted) and should be only half-filled. The best sizes range
from 8 to 11 ounces.

Finally, a few tips on taking care of your glasses. Wash
them as soon as possible after use, in warm water with plenty
of soap. After washing rinse them in scalding hot water and
dry them with a lint-free towel or let them drain dry. If the
rinse water was hot enough you shouldn't have any trouble
with the glasses water-spotting.

Mixing Tips:

To mix a drink properly you have to get all the ingredients in proper proportion, and drink recipes often call for
unusual measures. Below are some of the most common.

Dash: A dash is 1/8 teaspoon. There are "dash" pour-
ers, but they are seldom accurate, and things which
are poured in dashes are usually pretty potent in flavor, and a dash-and-a-half where a dash is called for
can make for an ugly tasting drink.

Teaspoon: 1/3 of a tablespoon, or 1/6 ounce. Use a

measuring teaspoon, not a barspoon.

Tablespoon: 3 teaspoons or 1/2 ounce.

Pony: 1 ounce.

Jigger: 1 1/2 ounces, the standard measure for mixing drinks.

Split: 8 ounces, 1/2 pint, the contents of 1 measuring cup.

Pint: 16 ounces, 1/2 quart, 2 standard measuring cups. Read the labels of "pint" bottles very carefully, as they may actually be half-a-fifth (12 ounces) or some other strange measures.

Fifth: 25.6 ounces, 4/5 quart, 1/5 gallon.

Quart: 32 ounces, 2 pints, 4 measuring cups, 1/4 gallon.

Magnum: 52 ounces. The double-size champagne bottle.

Half-Gallon: 64 ounces.

Remember that a fifth will provide seventeen jigger-size drinks, and a quart will make twenty-one drinks.

Chilling Glasses:

Store the glasses in the freezer for one hour or bury them in cracked ice. Necessary for all cocktail-glass drinks.

Frosting Glasses:

Dip the glasses in water and immediately place in the freezer for three hours.

Sugar-Frosting Glasses:

Rub the top quarter-inch of the rim, inside and out, with a piece of lemon or orange, then dip the glass into superfine sugar. For drinks with a coffee liqueur base moisten the rim with coffee liqueur, then dip into a mixture of superfine sugar and instant coffee.

Shaking:

Put the ice in the shaker first so the ingredients are cooled as they are poured in. Really shake it, don't rock it, so that the drink will have a creamy head, then wash the shaker immediately after use.

Stirring:

To keep them clear drinks such as martinis, manhattans, Rob Roys, gimlets, etc. should be stirred, not shaken. Except where carbonated materials (club soda, 7 Up, etc.) are used the drink should be stirred at least twenty times before serving. Stir carbonated drinks only two or three times.

Flaming:

Whenever you have to set fire to a drink (usually brandy), preheat a teaspoon of the liquid first over an open flame, light it, then slowly pour it into the rest of the liquid.

7. WHISKEY OR WHISKY?

The Scots and the Irish are not noted for harmony either as nations or as individuals. Despite their common heritage and their shared Gaelic tongue, they are at odds on just about everything except for the long and deeply treasured hatred of the English. They both claim to have invented the bagpipes; they both apparently wore clan tartans first and, of course, they both invented whiskey—or is it whisky? They can't even agree on the spelling. The Irish spell the word with an "e" and the Scots spell it without. Perhaps this is attributable to the latter's innate thrift. This spelling pattern followed them across the Atlantic. Canada, which was heavily colonized by the Scots, spells it whisky, and in the United States, where an Irishman or two has been known to settle, distillers opted for the more elaborate version.

Whiskey, however it is spelled, is a spirit distilled from grain. Any one of a number of different cereals is first fermented in pulp form known as mash, and this is then distilled into the final product. There are six distinct branches of the whiskey family. Three domestic and three imported. From the United States come bourbon, rye and corn whiskeys, and from outside come Scotch, Irish and Canadian. All follow the same basic distillation process, but different grains used for the initial fermentation and regional peculiarities in storing and aging methods give each its distinctive character.

Bourbon is, of course, the most important domestic whiskey form. Its name dates back to a period when liquor was known by the region from which it emanated and the Bourbon County of Kentucky was famous for a particular type of corn-rye-based whiskey. By the end of the last century, bourbon had been adopted as a generic term. Traditionally, the proportions of the two grains were entirely up to the individual distiller, but today this has been to a large extent standardized with a ratio of approximately fifty-one percent corn to forty-nine percent rye, wheat, oats and barley.

Rye whiskey, as the name suggests, was originally distilled from a mash consisting solely of rye, but today this has been lowered to as little as fifty-five percent with the balance made up from any number of other grains.

The traditional method of distilling corn whiskey, on the other hand, has survived almost unaltered from the days when it was a cottage industry. The mash is almost one hundred percent corn, with just enough malted barley added to facilitate fermentation. That is why, while some bourbons taste like rye and vice-versa, corn whiskey has retained its very distinctive taste and aroma.

Of the imported whiskeys, Scotch outsells the others by

a wide, and increasing, margin. Pure malt Scotch is made from malted barley by literally hundreds of tiny distilleries scattered throughout the highlands and islands of Scotland. This fine drink is never seen by the average Scotch drinker. True, some single malts, as they are called, are bottled and sold on the open market, but they are expensive and rare outside of their country of origin. The vast majority of the malt whisky produced by these craftsmen is sold to the major commercial distilleries, where it is blended with factory-produced grain whisky and becomes any one of the hundreds of proprietery brands of Scotch which adorn the liquor store shelves. These blended whiskys vary enormously in quality, but none compare with the smoky delicacy of a true single malt. If you are lucky enough to come across such a prize, savor it; don't use it for cocktails—that would be tantamount to sacrilege. If you don't happen to enjoy it, you can bet your life that it won't be long before a true Scot will happen by and sniff it out.

Irish whiskey is produced by the same method as Scotch, but, despite the fact that it enjoys a substantial following in parts of the United States, it does not compare in quality with the finest Scotch. This is explained in part by the difference in water used by the distillers of the two countries, but in truth it has more to do with the innate superiority of the distillers and blenders of Scotland, who combine as many as fifty different malts in a single blend to acquire the desired effect.

Canadian whiskey sells in this country in quite large quantities, but one suspects that that has more to do with tastes developed during prohibition and the convenient location of its country of origin than any particular merit of the spirit itself. It tends to be thin-bodied and rather watery to a Scotch drinker, but as such makes a good base for delicate cocktails.

The cocktails listed below have been split into sections. It is clearly nonsense to use expensive imported liquor if its taste is to be smothered with other ingredients. Most of the very elaborate cocktails, therefor, stipulate bourbon as a base. This is not to say that Scotch, rye or Canadian could not be used just as well. It is largely a matter of common sense. You can tell by looking at the list of ingredients how much whiskey flavor will come through, and when that has been realized you can choose your base according to taste, budget and availability.

WHISKEY DRINKS AND COCKTAILS

Old Favorites

BOURBON AND SODA
2 oz bourbon
6 oz club soda
Pour over two ice cubes into a 12 oz chimney glass and stir. The proportions and measure of this drink can, of course, be varied considerably according to taste, but the above is a good rule of thumb.

BOURBON AND WATER
Pour 1½ to 2 oz of bourbon over ice cubes in a chimney glass and serve a small pitcher of cold water alongside to allow the individual to mix his drink to taste.

BOURBON MIST
3 oz bourbon

Fill an old-fashioned glass three-quarters full of crushed ice; add bourbon and a twist of lemon peel.

JOHN COLLINS
1 oz bourbon
1 oz lemon juice
½ oz sugar syrup
½ lime
Club soda
Pour lemon juice syrup and whiskey into a highball glass filled with ice cubes; squeeze in lime juice, retaining skin; top up with soda; stir; decorate with lime shell and serve with two straws.

MANHATTAN
Every barman has his own idea of what makes a great Manhattan. None is right and none is wrong. It's just a matter of personal taste. Here are a few versions. Try them and stick to the one you like. If you don't like any of them, experiment!

MANHATTAN 1
1 oz bourbon or rye
½ oz Italian vermouth
1 dash bitters
Stir with ice cubes; strain into a chilled cocktail glass and decorate with a cherry.

MANHATTAN 2
1 oz rye
¾ oz Italian vermouth
1 dash orange bitters

Stir with ice cubes and strain into a chilled cocktail glass.

MANHATTAN (dry)
As above but use French vermouth.

MANHATTAN ON THE ROCKS
1½ oz bourbon
½ oz Italian vermouth
1 dash bitters
Stir with ice cubes; strain into an old-fashioned glass over fresh ice cubes and decorate with a cherry.

MANHATTAN ON THE ROCKS (dry)
As above using French vermouth.

OLD-FASHIONED
Old-fashioned comes in even more profuse varieties than Manhattans. Again we have listed a few.

OLD-FASHIONED 1
1½ oz bourbon or rye
½ sugar cube
1 dash bitters
Club soda
Mix the sugar and the bitters in an old-fashioned glass; add whiskey together with a couple of ice cubes; stir gently and decorate with a cherry and a slice of orange.

OLD-FASHIONED 2
1½ oz bourbon
½ sugar cube
2 dashes bitters

1 dash curacao
Mix the sugar and the bitters in an old-fashioned glass; add the whiskey and curacao; a twist of lemon, and decorate with a slice of orange.

SCOTCH AND SODA
2 oz Scotch
6 oz club soda
Pour whiskey into a chimney glass with two ice cubes and stir.

SCOTCH AND WATER
Serve as bourbon and water.

Some Fancier Bourbon Cocktails

ALLIES AND AXIS
½ oz bourbon
1 teaspoon Italian vermouth
1 teaspoon French vermouth
1 generous squeeze of lemon juice
1 egg white
Shake well with cracked ice and strain into a well-chilled cocktail glass.

BLACK EYE
1½ oz bourbon (blended rye or Canadian can be substituted)
1½ oz sloe gin
Stir well with crushed ice and strain into a 3-oz cocktail glass; decorate with a cherry.

BOSTON SOUR
2 oz bourbon

1 teaspoon powdered sugar
½ lemon
1 egg white
Pour whiskey and sugar into a cocktail shaker; add the juice of half a lemon and an egg white; shake well with cracked ice and pour into a highball glass. Add two ice cubes; top up with club soda and decorate with a slice of lemon and a cherry.

BOURBON LEMON
Juice of 1 lemon
Juice of 1 lime
3 teaspoons sugar
2½ oz bourbon
1 dash grenadine
Soda water
Shake well with ice cubes and pour into a chimney glass almost filled with shaved ice. Top up with soda water; decorate with orange and cherry; serve with two straws.

CAPTAIN COLLINS
2 oz bourbon
Juice of one lime
½ oz grenadine
Soda water
Shake with ice cubes; strain into chimney glass half filled with ice cubes; top up with soda water and stir.

CREOLE LADY
1¼ oz bourbon
1¼ oz Madeira
1 teaspoon grenadine

Stir with cracked ice, strain into a cocktail glass and decorate with a green cherry.

COMEDY COCKTAIL
2½ oz bourbon
1 teaspoon white creme de menthe
½ teaspoon curacao
1 dash bitters
¼ teaspoon sugar
Shake well with cracked ice and strain into a cocktail glass.

KING COLE COCKTAIL
1 slice pineapple
1 slice orange
1 teaspoon sugar
2 oz bourbon
Cut fruit into small pieces; mix with sugar in an old-fashioned glass; add whiskey and one ice cube; stir.

KING GEORGE
½ oz bourbon
½ oz gin
½ oz white creme de cacao
½ oz lemon juice
Shake well with ice cubes and strain into a large saucer glass.

LINSTEAD COCKTAIL
1 oz bourbon
1 oz pineapple juice
½ teaspoon powdered sugar
¼ teaspoon pernod
¼ teaspoon lemon juice

Shake well with cracked ice and strain into a cocktail glass.

MAPLE LEAF
1 oz bourbon
1 teaspoon maple syrup
Juice of half lemon
Shake well with ice cubes and strain into a chilled cocktail glass.

NEW ORLEANS
2 oz bourbon
3 dashes herbsaint
2 dashes bitters
1 teaspoon sugar syrup
Shake well with ice cubes; strain into chilled cocktail glass and a twist of lemon.

PINCHER
1 oz bourbon
½ oz lemon juice
½ oz orange juice
1 generous dash syrup
Mix with ice cubes in an electric mixer; pour into an old-fashioned glass and decorate with slices of orange, lemon and a sprig of fresh mint. Serve with two straws.

NEOPOLITAN
1½ oz bourbon
½ oz Italian vermouth
1 dash bitters
Stir with ice cubes and strain into a chilled cocktail glass; decorate with cherry.

RATTLESNAKE
1½ oz bourbon
1 teaspoon lemon juice
½ teaspoon sugar
¼ teaspoon absinthe substitute
1 egg white
Shake with cracked ice and strain into a chilled cocktail glass.

SWEET AND SAVAGE
1 oz bourbon
1 oz dry vermouth
¼ oz dubonnet
¼ oz orange juice
Shake well with cracked ice and strain into a chilled cocktail glass.

WAIKIKI
1 oz bourbon
¼ oz triple sec
½ oz lemon juice
1 teaspoon grenadine
Mix with shaved ice in an electric blender and pour into large saucer-shaped glass.

Fancy Scotch Cocktails

BLACK WATCH
2 oz Scotch
1 oz Kahlua
Club soda
Pour scotch and Kahlua over ice cubes in an old-fashioned

glass; add a splash of soda; stir and decorate with a twist of lemon.

BEADLESTONE
1¼ oz Scotch
1¼ oz dry vermouth
Stir well with cracked ice and strain into a chilled cocktail glass.

BLOOD AND GUTS
1 oz Scotch
½ oz orange juice
½ oz cherry brandy
½ oz sweet vermouth
Shake well with cracked ice and strain into a chilled cocktail glass.

CAMERON HIGHLANDER
½ oz Scotch
½ oz Irish
Juice of ½ lemon
Generous dash of orange bitters
Shake well with cracked ice and strain into a chilled cocktail glass.

FLYING SCOTSMAN
1½ oz Scotch
1½ oz Italian vermouth
1 dash bitters
¼ teaspoon sugar syrup
Stir well with ice cubes and strain into chilled cocktail glass.

MAMIE TAYLOR
2 oz Scotch
Juice of half lime
Ginger ale
Pour lime and Scotch over ice cubes in a chimney glass; top up with ginger ale and stir.

MACDUFF COCKTAIL
1 oz Scotch
½ oz dry vermouth
½ oz grapefruit juice
Stir well with cracked ice and strain into a cocktail glass.

MORNING GLORY
2 oz Scotch
½ teaspoon absinthe substitute
White of 1 egg
1 teaspoon fine sugar
Juice of 1 lime
Shake well with cracked ice; strain into a highball glass and top up with carbonated water.

ROB ROY
2 oz Scotch
1 oz Italian vermouth
1 dash bitters
Stir with ice cubes and strain into a chilled cocktail glass; decorate with cherry.

ROBBIE BURNS COCKTAIL
1½ oz Scotch
½ oz Italian vermouth

1 dash orange bitters
1 dash pernod
Stir with ice cubes and strain into a chilled cocktail glass.

RUSTY NAIL
1 oz Scotch
1 oz Drambuie
Stir well with cracked ice and strain into a cocktail glass.

SCOTCH COLLINS
1 oz Scotch
1 oz lemon juice
½ oz sugar syrup
Juice of half lime
Club soda
Stir well in a highball glass with ice cubes; top up with soda and decorate with a slice of lime.

SPORREN
1 oz Scotch
½ oz sloe gin
1 dash bitters
Juice of half lemon
Shake well with ice cubes and strain into a chilled cocktail glass.

STARBOARD LIGHT
2 oz Scotch
2 teaspoons honey
½ oz passion fruit juice
1 egg white
Mix in an electric blender with one handful of crushed ice.

Pour into a chimney glass; add ice cubes and decorate with fresh mint.

THISTLE COCKTAIL
1½ oz sweet vermouth
1 oz Scotch
2 dashes bitters
Shake well with cracked ice and strain into a chilled cocktail glass.

Irish and Rye

Many of the cocktails described above can be made with Irish or rye whiskey. There's no hard and fast rule. Try them; it's just a matter of taste. But here's a few recipes which are specifically designed to use the minor-league whiskeys as a base.

IRISH CHEER
2 oz Irish whiskey
½ oz Italian vermouth
Stir with cracked ice and strain into a chilled cocktail glass.

SHILLELAGH
1½ oz Irish whiskey
½ oz sloe gin
½ oz Bacardi rum
Juice of half lemon
1 teaspoon sugar
2 slices peach
Fresh raspberries and stawberries
Mix first six ingredients in a cocktail shaker with ice cubes;

strain into a chilled punch glass; decorate with berries and a red cherry.

RYE HIGHBALL
2 oz rye whiskey
Ginger ale
Pour whiskey over a single ice cube in a highball glass; top up with ginger ale and stir gently.

GOING THROUGH THE RYE
2 oz rye whiskey
1 teaspoon sugar syrup
1 dash bitters
Stir well with ice cubes; strain into a chilled cocktail glass and decorate with a cherry.

8. VODKA

While lovers of single malt whiskeys and fine brandies contemplate their chosen and beloved amber liquids in rapt anticipation, lovers of vodka simply *drink*. The reason is quite simple: there's nothing for them to contemplate. To fall within the legal definition, vodka must be colorless, odorless, and lack any distinctive flavor.

There is a common misconception that vodka is distilled from potatoes. While it is true that a small proportion of the cheapest Russian vodka is produced by this method, ninety-nine percent of the vodka consumed in this country is distilled from grain. It is, in fact, little more than pure alcohol diluted with water to a strength at which it can safely be consumed. It's hardly an exciting prospect for the discerning palate, but vodka has found its niche with the cocktail boom. Its almost total lack of character suddenly became an asset rather than a handicap. It will mix with

literally anything, and the resulting cocktail will taste just as good or as bad as the sum total of ingredients that go into it. In consequence, vodka has boomed—from a very small percentage of all the liquor sold in the United States twenty years ago, to an astonishing twenty-plus percent of the total market today.

Imported vodkas have a certain snob appeal, and one is assured frequently that a true vodka drinker can tell various brands apart, but for your average cocktail drinker they're a plain waste of good money. To mix twelve-dollar Polish vodka with tomato juice and then sprinkle it liberally with worcestershire and Tobasco is not chic; it's dumb. Spend $4.00 and get a fifth of domestic from your supermarket, or better yet spend the $12.00 and get three fifths.

VODKA COCKTAILS

BALALAIKA
1½ oz vodka
1½ oz cointreau
1½ oz lemon juice
Shake well with cracked ice and strain into a dish glass; decorate with a twist of lemon.

BLACK MAGIC
1½ oz vodka
¾ oz expresso coffee liqueur
Dash of lemon juice
Stir and serve in old-fashioned glass with cubes of ice and twist of lemon peel.

BLACK RUSSIAN

1½ oz vodka
¾ oz Kahlua (coffee liqueur)
Pour on ice cubes in old-fashioned glass.

BLOODY MARY
2 oz vodka
2 oz tomato juice
½ teaspoon lemon juice
½ teaspoon worcestershire sauce
Salt, black pepper, celery salt
1 or 2 dashes Tobasco sauce
Shake together with cracked ice and strain into an old-fashioned glass, half filled with cubes.

BLUE MONDAY
1½ oz vodka
¾ oz triple sec
1 dash blue vegetable coloring
Stir well with cracked ice and strain into 3-oz cocktail glass.

CAPE CODDER
1½ oz vodka or imported rum
3 oz cranberry juice
Juice ½ lime (if desired)
May be served on the rocks in old-fashioned glass or in 8-oz highball glass with cubes of ice and carbonated water. Stir.

CLAM AND TOMATO COCKTAIL
1½ oz vodka
1 oz clam juice
3 oz tomato juice
Shake well with cracked ice; strain and serve on the rocks in

large old-fashioned glass.

CYCLONE
3 oz vodka
1 oz dry vermouth
1 teaspoon pernod
Shake well with cracked ice and strain into a cocktail glass; garnish with a lemon rind.

CANNONBALL
1 oz vodka
1 oz Galliano
2 oz vanilla ice cream
Shake well with cracked ice and strain into a chilled cocktail glass; decorate with a cherry.

FLYING GRASSHOPPER
¾ oz creme de menthe (green)
¾ oz creme de cacao (white)
¾ oz vodka
Stir well with cracked ice and strain into 3-oz cocktail glass.

HEADLESS HORSEMAN
2 oz vodka
3 dashes bitters
Pour into 12-oz Tom Collins glass; add several cubes of ice; fill with dry ginger ale and stir. Decorate with slice of orange.

KANGAROO COCKTAIL
1½ oz vodka
¾ oz dry vermouth
Stir well with cracked ice and strain into 3-oz cocktail glass.

Serve with twist of lemon peel.

KOTUKA
1 oz vodka
½ oz Benedictine
1 dash lime juice cordial
3 dashes grenadine
Shake well with cracked ice and strain into 5-oz champagne glass. Garnish with maraschino cherry.

KRETCHMA
1 oz vodka
1 oz creme de cacao
½ oz lemon juice
1 dash grenadine
Shake well with cracked ice and strain into 3-oz cocktail glass.

LUCKY DIP
2 oz vodka
1 oz creme de bananes
1 oz lemon cordial
½ white of one egg
Shake well with cracked ice and strain into 5-oz champagne glass.

MAIDEN'S BLUSH
2 oz vodka
1 oz grenadine
½ oz Galliano
1 oz fresh lemon juice
½ white of one egg

Shake well with cracked ice and strain into 5-oz champagne glass. Garnish with maraschino cherry

MOSCOW MULE
1½ oz vodka
Juice of ½ lime
Put into a copper mug and add ice cubes; fill with ginger beer. Drop lime in mug to decorate.

PINK PUSSY CAT
1½ oz vodka or gin
Using 7-oz highball glass almost filled with shaved ice, fill balance of glass with pineapple or grapefruit juice. Add dash of grenadine for color and stir.

PINK ELEPHANT
¾ oz vodka
¾ oz Galliano
¾ oz creme de noyaux or almond liqueur
¾ oz fresh orange juice
¾ oz fresh cream
1 dash grenadine
Shake well with cracked ice and strain into 5-oz champagne glass. Sprinkle cinnamon on top.

QUEEN BEE
1 oz vodka
½ oz Galliano
½ oz pure honey
2 oz fresh cream
Shake well with cracked ice and strain into 5-oz champagne glass. Garnish with maraschino cherry.

RUSSIAN BEAR COCKTAIL
1 oz vodka
½ oz creme de cacao
½ oz sweet cream
Stir well with cracked ice and strain into 3-oz cocktail glass.

RUSSIAN COCKTAIL
¾ oz creme de cacao
¾ oz gin
¾ oz vodka
Shake well with cracked ice and strain into 3-oz cocktail glass.

SCREWDRIVER
Put 2 or 3 cubes of ice into 6-oz glass. Add 2 oz vodka. Fill balance of glass with orange juice and stir.

TASTE OF HONEY
1 oz vodka
1½ oz advokaat
¾ oz Galliano
Shake well with cracked ice and pour with ice into 10-oz highball glass. Top up with lemonade. Garnish with maraschino cherry. Add straw and swizzle stick.

TOVARICH COCKTAIL
1½ oz vodka
¾ oz kummel
Juice of ½ lime
Shake well with cracked ice and strain into 3-oz cocktail glass.

VODKA DAISY
Juice ½ lemon
½ teaspoon powdered sugar
1 teaspoon grenadine
2 oz vodka
Shake well with cracked ice and strain into stein or 8-oz metal cup. Add cube of ice and decorate with fruit.

VODKA GIBSON
3 oz vodka
1 oz dry vermouth
Stir gently with cracked ice and strain into 5-oz champagne glass. Garnish with a white pickled pearl onion.

VODKA MARTINI (dry)
4 oz vodka
Dash dry vermouth
Stir gently with cracked ice and strain into 5-oz champagne glass. Garnish with twist of lemon rind.

VODKA GRASSHOPPER COCKTAIL
¾ oz vodka
¾ oz creme de menthe (green)
¾ oz creme de cacao (white)
Shake well with cracked ice; strain into 3-oz cocktail glass.

VODKA GYPSY COCKTAIL
1½ oz vodka
¾ oz Benedictine
1 dash bitters
Stir well with cracked ice and strain into 3-oz cocktail glass.

9. GIN

Despite its origin in Holland, gin is a beverage most commonly associated with the English. It has a long and rather unsavory association with the British working class, to whom, during the seventeenth through the nineteenth centuries, it offered the only available cheap high. Somehow it gained the nickname "mother's ruin," reflecting its reputation as a woman's drink, a reputation which it retains in England to this day. It is still considered slightly effeminate for a man to order a gin and tonic in an English pub.

Second only to vodka, gin is the most basic of all the liquors. Distillers have never aspired to, let alone achieved, the epicurean heights of their counterparts in the world of Scotch and brandy. Gin is merely grain mash distilled down and then distilled for a second time with aromatics such as juniper and coriander. Different additives during this second stage give each brand of gin its slight but definite character.

Gins are generally described as either sweet or dry. The best London gins are dry, and are favored by true gin drinkers, who generally mix them with quinine water. Most American domestic gins are slightly sweeter and are more suitable for use as a cocktail base.

Occasionally one will find fruit gins on sale. These are produced by adding any one of several fruits instead of the usual aromatics during the second distillation stage. The most common of these are orange and lemon gin, but they are, for the most part, confined to and favored in Europe.

Dutch gin is seldom seen outside its country of origin. It is usually sold in tall stone bottles and has an awesome flavor which is very much an acquired taste and totally unsuitable as a cocktail base.

For most of the cocktails listed below, use an inexpensive brand of gin. No one will ever know the difference.

GIN DRINKS

ARTILLERY
2 oz dry gin
1 oz sweet vermouth
2 dashes Angostura bitters
Stir well with cracked ice and strain into 5-oz champagne glass. Garnish with twist of lemon rind.

BARBARY COAST
1 oz dry gin
1 oz Scotch
1 oz creme de cacao
1 oz fresh cream
Shake well with cracked ice and strain into an old-fashioned

glass.

BEAUTY SPOT COCKTAIL
1 tcaspoon orange juice
½ oz sweet vermouth
½ oz dry vermouth
1 oz gin
Shake well with cracked ice and strain into 3-oz cocktail glass, with a dash of grenadine in bottom of glass.

BEE'S KNEES
1 oz gin
1 teaspoon honey
Juice of ½ lemon
Shake well with cracked ice and strain into 5-oz champagne glass.

BLUE MOON
1½ oz gin
¾ oz creme de yvette
Stir well with cracked ice and strain into 3-oz cocktail glass. Add twist of lemon peel and drop in glass.

BRONX
1 oz gin
½ oz dry vermouth
½ oz sweet vermouth
Juice ¼ orange
Shake well with cracked ice and strain into 3-oz cocktail glass. Serve with slice of orange.

BLUE LAGOON

2 oz dry gin
1 oz blue curacao
Dash lime juice cordial
Dash Angostura bitters
Shake well with cracked ice and strain into 5-oz champagne glass. Garnish with a cherry.

CARDINAL
1½ oz gin
1½ oz campari
1½ oz dry vermouth
Shake with cracked ice and strain into 5-oz champagne glass. Garnish with twist of lemon rind.

DAY DREAM ISLAND
2 oz dry gin
1 oz Galliano
½ oz blue curacao
½ oz fresh orange juice
½ white of egg
Shake well with cracked ice and strain into 5-oz champagne glass. Garnish with maraschino cherry.

DRY MARTINI NO. 1
4 oz dry gin
Dash dry vermouth
Stir gently with cracked ice and strain into 5-oz champagne glass. Garnish with twist of lemon rind or olive.

DRY MARTINI NO. 2
2 oz dry gin
1 oz dry vermouth

Stir gently with cracked ice and strain into 5-oz champagne glass. Garnish with twist of lemon rind or olive.

FALLEN ANGEL
Juice of 1 lemon or ½ lime
1½ oz gin
1 dash bitters
½ teaspoon creme de menthe (white)
Shake well with cracked ice and strain into 3-oz cocktail glass. Serve with a cherry.

FOG HORN
1 cube of ice
Juice of ½ lime
1½ oz gin
Fill 8-oz highball glass with ginger ale and stir. Leave lime in glass.

FRENCH 75
Juice of 1 lemon
2 teaspoons powdered sugar
Stir well in 12-oz Tom Collins glass. Then add 1 cube of ice, 2 oz gin and fill with champagne and stir gently. Decorate with slice of lemon, orange and a cherry. Serve with straws.

GIMLET
Juice 1 lime
1 teaspoon powdered sugar
1½ oz gin
Shake well with cracked ice and strain into 4-oz cocktail glass.

GIN AND BITTERS
Put ½ teaspoon bitters into 3-oz cocktail glass and revolve glass until it is entirely coated with the bitters. Then fill with gin. No ice is used in this drink.

GIN AND IT (English)
2 oz gin
1 oz sweet vermouth
Stir. No ice is used in this drink. Serve in 3-oz cocktail glass.

GIN AND TONIC
2 oz gin
Cube of ice
Fill glass with quinine water and stir. Use 12-oz Tom Collins glass.

GIN SLING
Dissolve 1 teaspoon powdered sugar in 1 teaspoon water and juice of ½ lemon.
2 oz gin
2 cubes of ice
Serve in old-fashioned cocktail glass and stir. Twist of orange peel and drop in glass.

GIN SOUR
Juice of ½ lemon
½ teaspoon powdered sugar
2 oz gin
Shake well with cracked ice and strain into 6-oz sour glass. Decorate with a half-slice of lemon and a cherry.

GIN SWIZZLE

Into 12-oz Tom Collins glass put:
Juice 1 lime
1 teaspoon powdered sugar
2 oz carbonated water
Fill glass with shaved ice and stir thoroughly with swizzle stick. Then add:
2 dashes bitters
2 oz gin
Fill with carbonated water and serve with swizzle stick in glass, allowing individual to do final stirring.

HAWAIIAN

2 oz dry gin
1 oz pineapple juice
1 dash orange bitters
1 egg white
Shake well with cracked ice and strain into 5-oz champagne glass.

HEAVEN'S HONEY

1 oz dry gin
1½ oz advokaat
¾ oz Galliano
Shake well with cracked ice and pour into 5-oz champagne glass.

HONOLULU

1 dash bitters
¼ teaspoon orange juice
¼ teaspoon pineapple juice
¼ teaspoon lemon juice
½ teaspoon powdered sugar

1½ oz gin
Shake well with cracked ice and strain into 3-oz cocktail glass.

HULA-HULA
2 oz dry gin
1 oz fresh orange juice
1 dash curacao
Shake well with cracked ice and strain into 5-oz champagne glass.

JOHN COLLINS
Juice ½ lemon
1 teaspoon powdered sugar
2 oz gin
Shake well with cracked ice and strain into 12-oz Tom Collins glass. Add several cubes of ice; fill with carbonated water and stir. Decorate with slice of orange, lemon and a cherry. Serve with straws.

KNICKERBOCKER
2 oz dry gin
1 oz dry vermouth
1 dash sweet vermouth
Stir well with cracked ice and strain into 5-oz champagne glass. Garnish with a twist of lemon rind.

LADY LEON
1 oz gin
1 oz dry vermouth
1 oz orange curacao
1 oz Galliano

Stir well with cracked ice and strain into 5-oz champagne glass. Garnish with a twist of lemon rind.

MAIDEN'S DELIGHT
2 oz dry gin
4 dashes curacao
4 dashes grenadine
1-2 dashes fresh lemon juice
Shake well with cracked ice and strain into 5-oz champagne glass.

MAIDEN'S BLUSH
2 oz dry gin
1 oz pernod
1 teaspoon grenadine
Stir well with cracked ice and strain into 5-oz champagne glass. Garnish with a twist of lemon rind.

MAIDEN'S PRAYER
1½ oz dry gin
1½ oz cointreau
½ oz fresh lemon juice
½ oz fresh orange juice
Stir well with cracked ice and strain into 5-oz champagne glass.

MERRY WIDOW
1¼ oz gin
1¼ oz dry vermouth
½ teaspoon Benedictine
½ teaspoon absinthe substitute
1 dash orange bitters

Stir well with cracked ice and strain into 3-oz cocktail glass. Add twist of lemon peel and drop in glass.

MONKEY GLAND

2 oz dry gin
1 oz fresh orange juice
½ oz pernod
½ oz grenadine
Shake with cracked ice and strain into 5-oz champagne glass. Garnish with a twist of orange rind.

NEGRONIS

¾ oz gin
¾ oz campari bitters
¾ oz sweet or dry vermouth
Shake well with cracked ice and strain into old-fashioned cocktail glass. May also be served over ice cubes in 8-oz highball glass adding carbonated water and stirring.

ORANGE BLOSSOM

2 oz dry gin
1 oz sweet vermouth
1 oz cointreau
Stir with cracked ice and strain into 5-oz champagne glass. Garnish with a cherry.

PARADISE

1 oz dry gin
1 oz apricot brandy
1 oz fresh orange or lemon juice
Stir well with cracked ice and strain into 5-oz champagne glass. Garnish with twist of lemon or orange rind.

SALTY DOG
Fill 12-oz Tom Collins glass almost full with shaved ice or ice cubes and add:
2 oz gin
2 oz grapefruit, lemon or lime juice
¼ teaspoon salt
Stir well.

ST. VINCENT
1 oz dry gin
1 oz Galliano
1 oz fresh cream
¼ oz grenadine
Shake with cracked ice and strain into 5-oz champagne glass. Garnish with a cherry.

SINGAPORE SLING
Juice ½ lemon
1 teaspoon powdered sugar
2 oz gin
½ oz cherry flavored brandy
Shake well with cracked ice and strain into 12-oz Tom Collins glass. Add ice cubes and fill with carbonated water; stir. Decorate with fruits in season and serve with straws.

SUBMARINE
2 oz dry gin
1 oz dubonnet
1 oz dry vermouth
1 dash Angostura bitters
Stir well with cracked ice and strain into 5-oz champagne glass.

SWEET MARTINI
2 oz dry gin
2 oz sweet vermouth
Stir gently with cracked ice and strain into 5-oz champagne glass. Garnish with a cherry.

WHITE LADY
2 oz gin
1 oz cointreau
1 oz fresh lemon juice
1 teaspoon of egg white
Shake well with cracked ice and strain into a 5-oz champagne glass. Garnish with a maraschino cherry.

WILD OATS
2 oz dry gin
2 oz kirsch
Dash fresh lemon juice
Dash apricot brandy
Shake well with cracked ice and strain into 5-oz champagne glass.

YOLANDA
1 oz dry gin
1 oz brandy
2 oz sweet vermouth
Dash grenadine
Dash pernod
Stir well with cracked ice and strain into a 5-oz champagne glass.

"*You all know that game where you try to pin the tail on the donkey. Well, this is a slightly new version!*"

10. RUM

Above all other drinks, rum conjures up a host of color-ful associations—the navy, pirates, uncharted islands in the Caribbean laden with treasure. Indeed, it deserves a great deal of this glamor. For centuries it was the tradition in the British Royal Navy to give each man his daily quota of rum, perhaps because it was the only way of making the appalling living conditions tolerable. And of course it does come from the tropics. All rum is distilled from sugar or a sugar-associated material and therefor, by definition, the tropics are the only region where the raw materials for the spirit are available.

Today there are about a dozen different types of rum on the market. Unlike the different whiskeys, however, they vary in character rather than basic nature. For the purposes of the home bartender, they can be considered to fall under three broad headings. Dark rum, sometimes called navy rum, comes primarily from Jamaica. It is heavy and pungent, and very much an acquired taste. It is drunk to some extent in Britain, but seldom in the United States. It is too heavy to use as a base for any cocktail, and therefor can be discounted for our purposes. Then there is light rum, which comes from Puerto Rico. This is by far the most popular type in this country, with its light body and comparatively delicate flavor. It makes an excellent base for cocktails, giving them a hint of "rummy-ness" without overpowering the other ingredients. In between these two lies another range of rums—the medium rums—which are imported from the Virgin Islands and have a much stronger flavor. They make an excellent base for some cocktails, notably punches and daiquiris.

Again, it is a matter of taste. If you are a real rum drinker, you may prefer to substitute medium rum for light in some of the following recipes, and vice-versa.

RUM DRINKS

AMERICAN GROG
1 lump of sugar
Juice ¼ lemon
1½ oz rum
Fill hot whiskey glass with hot water and stir.

BANGER
1 oz white rum
½ oz Galliano
6 oz fresh orange juice
Pour into 10-oz highball glass half filled with cracked ice. Garnish with ½ slice orange.

BACARDI COCKTAIL
1½ oz Bacardi rum
Juice ½ lime
½ teaspoon grenadine
Shake well with cracked ice and strain into 3-oz cocktail glass.

BOLERO
1½ oz rum
¾ oz apple brandy
¼ teaspoon sweet vermouth
Stir well with cracked ice and strain into 3-oz cocktail glass.

CREAM PUFF
2 oz rum
1 oz sweet cream
½ teaspoon powdered sugar
Shake well with cracked ice and strain into 8-oz highball glass. Fill with carbonated water and stir.

CUBA LIBRE
Juice ½ lime
Drop rind in glass
2 oz rum
2 cubes of ice
Fill glass with any cola. Use 10-oz glass and stir well.

DAIQUIRI
Juice 1 lime
1 teaspoon powdered sugar
1½ oz rum

Shake well with cracked ice and strain into 3-oz cocktail glass.

DUNLOP
2 oz light rum
1 oz sherry
Dash Angostura bitters
Stir well with cracked ice and strain into 5-oz champagne glass.

EL PRESIDENTE COCKTAIL
Juice 1 lime
1 teaspoon pineapple juice
1 teaspoon grenadine
1½ oz rum
Shake well with cracked ice and strain into 3-oz cocktail glass.

EYE-OPENER
2 oz light rum
2 dashes creme de noyaux
2 dashes curacao
2 dashes pernod
1 teaspoon castor sugar
1 egg yolk
Shake well with cracked ice and strain into 5-oz champagne glass.

FAIR AND WARMER
2 oz light rum
1 oz sweet vermouth
2 dashes curacao

Stir well with cracked ice and strain into 5-oz champagne glass. Garnish with a twist of lemon rind.

FIREMAN'S SOUR
Juice 2 limes
½ teaspoon powdered sugar
½ oz grenadine
2 oz rum
Shake well with cracked ice and strain into Delmonico glass. Fill with carbonated water, if desired. Decorate with a half-slice of lemon and a cherry.

FROZEN DAIQUIRI
Juice 1 lime
1 teaspoon powdered sugar
2 oz rum
Agitate in electric mixer filled with shaved ice for about 2 minutes. Strain through coarse meshed strainer into 6-oz champagne glass.

HAVANA COCKTAIL
1¼ oz pineapple juice
½ teaspoon lemon juice
¾ oz rum
Shake well with cracked ice and strain into 3-oz cocktail glass.

KNICKERBOCKER SPECIAL
1 teaspoon raspberry syrup
1 teaspoon lemon juice
1 teaspoon orange juice
2 oz rum

½ teaspoon curacao
Shake well with cracked ice and strain into 4-oz cocktail glass. Decorate with small slice of pineapple.

LIGHT FINGERS
2 oz white rum
1 oz anisette
1 oz parfait amour
Stir gently with cracked ice and strain into 5-oz champagne glass. Pour dash of grenadine on top of cocktail.

MIAMI BEACH
3 oz light rum
1 oz cointreau
Dash fresh lemon juice
Shake well with cracked ice and strain into 5-oz champagne glass.

MAI-TAI
½ teaspoon powdered sugar
2 oz rum
1 oz curacao
½ oz orgeat or any almond flavored syrup
½ oz grenadine
½ oz fresh lime juice
Shake well with cracked ice and strain into large old-fashioned cocktail glass about 1/3 full with crushed ice. Decorate with maraschino cherry speared to wedge of preferably fresh pineapple. For a hair raiser top with a dash of 151 proof rum and for a real Hawaiian effect float an orchid on each drink. Serve with straws.

NAKED LADY
2 oz light rum
2 oz sweet vermouth
4 dashes apricot brandy
2 dashes grenadine
4 dashes fresh lemon juice
Shake well with cracked ice and strain into 5-oz champagne glass.

ORIENTAL PEARL
¼ oz white rum
¼ oz creme de cassis
½ oz cola
½ oz fresh cream
Shake well with cracked ice and strain into 5-oz champagne glass. Garnish with a maraschino cherry.

PALMETTO COCKTAIL
1¼ oz rum
1¼ oz dry vermouth
2 dashes bitters
Stir well with cracked ice and strain into 3-oz cocktail glass.

PINEAPPLE COCKTAIL
¾ oz pineapple juice
1½ oz rum
½ teaspoon lemon juice
Shake well with cracked ice and strain into 3-oz cocktail glass.

PLANTER'S PUNCH
2 oz dark rum
½ oz fresh lemon juice

"I try to wear dresses that are just as interesting in the back as they are in the front!"

1 oz lime juice cordial
1 oz grenadine
Dash Angostura bitters
1 oz fresh orange juice
Pour into a 10-oz highball glass half filled with cracked ice. Garnish with ½ slice lemon and ½ slice orange; add straw and swizzle stick.

PRESIDENTE
2 oz light rum
Juice of ½ orange
2 dashes grenadine
Shake well with cracked ice and strain into 5-oz champagne glass. Garnish with twist of orange rind.

QUAKER
¾ oz rum
¾ oz brandy
Juice ¼ lemon
2 teaspoons raspberry syrup
Shake well with cracked ice and strain into 3-oz cocktail glass.

ROBSON COCKTAIL
2 teaspoons lemon juice
½ oz orange juice
¼ oz grenadine
1 oz Jamaica rum
Shake well with cracked ice and strain into 3-oz cocktail glass.

RUM DAISY

Juice of ½ lemon
½ teaspoon powdered sugar
1 teaspoon raspberry syrup or grenadine
2 oz rum
Shake well with cracked ice and strain into stein or 8-oz metal cup. Add cube of ice and decorate with fruit.

RUM RICKEY
1 cube of ice
Juice ½ lime
1½ oz rum
Fill 8-oz highball glass with carbonated water and stir. Leave lime in glass.

RUM SOUR
Juice ½ lemon
½ teaspoon powdered sugar
2 oz rum
Shake well with cracked ice and strain into 6-oz sour glass. Decorate with a half-slice of lemon and a cherry.

RUM THING
1 oz white rum
1 oz dry vermouth
1 oz orange curacao
1 oz Galliano
Stir with cracked ice and strain into 5-oz champagne glass. Garnish with twist of orange rind.

SNOW WHITE
2 oz white rum
1 oz cointreau

1 oz fresh lemon juice
½ teaspoon white of egg
Shake well with cracked ice and strain into 5-oz champagne glass. Garnish with a maraschino cherry.

SNAKE BITE
2 oz white rum
2 oz creme de menthe
Shake with cracked ice and strain into 5-oz champagne glass. Garnish with a maraschino cherry.

SPANISH TOWN COCKTAIL
2 oz rum
1 teaspoon curacao
Stir well with cracked ice and strain into 3-oz cocktail glass.

STONE
½ oz rum
½ oz sweet vermouth
1 oz sherry wine
Stir well with cracked ice and strain into 3-oz cocktail glass.

SUSIE TAYLOR
Juice ½ lime
2 cubes of ice
2 oz rum
Fill 12-oz Tom Collins glass with ginger ale and stir gently.

THIRD RAIL
¾ oz rum
¾ oz apple brandy
¾ oz brandy

¼ teaspoon absinthe substitute
Stir well with cracked ice and strain into 3-oz cocktail glass.

TWILIGHT ZONE
2 oz white rum
1 oz creme de menthe
½ oz parfait amour
½ oz lime cordial
½ oz fresh cream
Shake well with cracked ice and strain into a 5-oz champagne glass. Garnish with a maraschino cherry.

WEDDING NIGHT
2 oz light rum
Juice of ½ lemon
2 egg whites
2 dashes Angostura bitters
Shake well with cracked ice and strain into 5-oz champagne glass.

X.Y.Z.
½ oz lemon juice
½ oz triple sec
1 oz rum
Shake well with cracked ice and strain into 3-oz cocktail glass.

ZAZARAC
¾ oz white rum
¾ oz rye whiskey
1 oz pernod
¾ oz sugar syrup

Dash Angostura bitters
Dash orange bitters
Shake with cracked ice and strain into a 5-oz champagne glass. Garnish with a twist of lemon rind.

ZOMBIE
1 oz unsweetened pineapple juice
Juice 1 lime
Juice 1 small orange
1 teaspoon powdered sugar
½ oz apricot flavored brandy
2½ oz rum
1 oz Jamaica rum
1 oz passion fruit juice may be added
Add cracked ice and agitate for full minute in electric mixing machine (if none available, shake very well in cocktail shaker), and strain into 14-oz frosted zombie glass. Decorate with square of pineapple and 1 green and 1 red cherry. Carefully float ½ oz 151 proof Demerara rum and then top with sprig of fresh mint dipped in powdered sugar. Serve with straws.

"Never saw a young fellow as proud of his wife as young Locke."

11. BRANDY

Brandy is, by tradition, a product of France, and to this day the finest examples of this spirit emanate from the French distilleries. The manufacturing process is not dissimilar to that used by whiskey distillers, except that the grain mash is replaced by fermented grapes distilled into a rich and potent liquor. Brandy can be and is produced using other fruits as a base—cherries, oranges, apples, peaches, apricots; the list is endless. But if you order a brandy without specifying the type, it will inevitably be a grape product.

The word Cognac is carelessly bandied about. Cognac is indeed a brandy, just as champagne is a wine. It differs in only one way. It comes from the Charente district in France, and only brandies from this area are correctly termed Cognac. Like the finest Scotch whiskey, true Cognac is aged in oak barrels and is a superb example of the blender's art.

BRANDY COCKTAILS

ALEXANDER COCKTAIL
1 oz creme de cacao
1 oz brandy
1 oz sweet cream
Shake well with cracked ice and strain into 4-oz cocktail glass.

AMERICAN BEAUTY
1 oz brandy
1 oz dry vermouth
1 oz fresh orange juice
1 dash creme de menthe
1 dash grenadine
Shake well with cracked ice and strain into 5-oz champagne glass. Top carefully with a little port.

BALTIMORE BRACER
1 oz anisette
1 oz brandy
White of 1 egg
Shake well with cracked ice and strain into 4-oz cocktail glass.

BETWEEN THE SHEETS
1 oz brandy
1 oz cointreau
1 oz white rum
1 teaspoon lemon juice
Shake well with cracked ice and strain into 5-oz champagne glass. Garnish with a twist of lemon rind.

BOMBAY
2 oz brandy
1 oz sweet vermouth
1 oz dry vermouth
2 dashes curacao
1 dash pernod
Stir well with cracked ice and strain into 5-oz champagne glass.

BRANDY COCKTAIL
2 oz brandy
¼ teaspoon simple syrup
2 dashes bitters
Twist of lemon peel
Stir well with cracked ice and strain into 3-oz cocktail glass.

BRANDY CRUSTA
Moisten the edge of 4-oz cocktail glass with lemon and dip into sugar. Cut the rind of half a lemon in a spiral, and place in glass.
1 teaspoon maraschino
1 dash bitters
1 teaspoon lemon juice
½ oz curacao
2 oz brandy
Stir above ingredients in mixing glass and strain into glass prepared as above. Add slice of orange.

BRANDY DAISY
2 oz brandy
1 oz fresh lemon juice
½ oz grenadine

Shake well with cracked ice and strain into 10-oz highball glass. Top up with soda water or lemonade. Garnish with sprig of mint, ½ slice of lemon, ½ slice of orange and maraschino cherry. Add straw and swizzle stick.

BRANDY FIZZ
Juice ½ lemon
1 teaspoon powdered sugar
2 oz brandy
Shake well with cracked ice and strain into 7-oz highball glass. Fill with carbonated water.

BRANDY FLIP
1 egg
1 teaspoon powdered sugar
1½ oz brandy
2 teaspoons sweet cream (if desired)
Shake well with cracked ice and strain into 5-oz flip glass. Grate a little nutmeg on top

BRANDY MANHATTAN
3 oz brandy
1 oz sweet vermouth
1 dash Angostura bitters
Stir gently with cracked ice and strain into 5-oz champagne glass. Garnish with maraschino cherry.

BRANDY OLD-FASHIONED
Place lump of sugar in old-fashioned glass. Sprinkle sugar with 2 dashes of Angostura bitters and stir with teaspoon until sugar dissolves. Garnish with half-slice of orange and lemon. Fill glass with ice cubes and add 2 oz brandy.

BRANDY VERMOUTH
3 oz brandy
1 oz sweet vermouth
1 dash Angostura bitters
Stir well with cracked ice and strain into 5-oz champagne glass.

CONTESSA
¾ oz brandy
¾ oz cointreau
¾ oz Galliano
¾ oz fresh orange juice
¾ oz fresh cream
Shake well with cracked ice and strain into 5-oz champagne glass. Garnish with maraschino cherry.

CLASSIC COCKTAIL
Juice of ¼ lemon
¼ oz curacao
¼ oz maraschino
1 oz brandy
Shake well with cracked ice and strain into 3-oz cocktail glass. Frost rim of glass by rubbing with lemon and dipping in powdered sugar.

COFFEE COCKTAIL
1 egg
1 teaspoon powdered sugar
1 oz port wine
1 oz brandy
Shake well with cracked ice and strain into 5-oz cocktail glass. Grate nutmeg on top.

CUBAN COCKTAIL
Juice of ½ lime or ½ lemon
½ oz apricot flavored brandy
1½ oz brandy
1 teaspoon imported rum
Shake well with cracked ice and strain into 3-oz cocktail glass.

HARVARD COCKTAIL
1½ oz brandy
¾ oz sweet vermouth
1 dash bitters
1 teaspoon grenadine
2 teaspoons lemon juice
Shake well with cracked ice and strain into 3-oz cocktail glass.

JAMAICA GRANITO
Small scoop of either lemon or orange sherbet
1½ oz brandy
1 oz curacao
Use 12-oz Tom Collins glass and fill balance with carbonated water and stir. Grate nutmeg on top.

LADY BE GOOD
2 oz brandy
1 oz white creme de menthe
1 oz sweet vermouth
Shake well with cracked ice and strain into 5-oz champagne glass.

OFF THE LEASH

3 oz brandy
1 oz sweet vermouth
Stir well with cracked ice and strain into a 5-oz champagne glass. Garnish with maraschino cherry.

OLYMPIC COCKTAIL
¾ oz orange juice
¾ oz curacao
¾ oz brandy
Shake well with cracked ice and strain into 3-oz cocktail glass.

PANAMA COCKTAIL
1 oz creme de cacao
1 oz sweet cream
1 oz brandy
Shake well with cracked ice and strain into 4-oz cocktail glass.

SIDECAR
2 oz brandy
1 oz cointreau
1 oz lemon juice
1 teaspoon white of egg
Shake well with cracked ice and strain into a 5-oz champagne glass. Garnish with a twist of lemon rind.

SINK OR SWIM
3 oz brandy
1 oz sweet vermouth
1 dash Angostura bitters
Stir well with cracked ice and strain into a 5-oz champagne

glass.

STINGER
2 oz brandy
2 oz white creme de menthe
Shake well with cracked ice and strain into 5-oz champagne glass.

THREE SISTERS
1½ oz brandy
1½ oz Galliano
1½ oz fresh orange juice
1 dash grenadine
Shake well with cracked ice and strain into 5-oz champagne glass. Garnish with maraschino cherry.

WHIP
½ oz dry vermouth
½ oz sweet vermouth
1¼ oz brandy
¼ teaspoon absinthe substitute
1 teaspoon curacao
Stir well with cracked ice and strain into 3-oz cocktail glass.

YOUNG MAN
3 oz brandy
1 oz sweet vermouth
2 dashes curacao
1 dash Angostura bitters
Stir well with cracked ice and strain into 5-oz champagne glass.

12. LIQUEURS AND CORDIALS

The vast and gaudy array of bottles which line the mirrored shelves of cocktail bars throughout the world owe much of their color to the liqueur manufacturers. Bright-colored contents are made even more eye-dazzling by a seemingly limitless inventiveness in packaging. Round bottles, square bottles, bottles with twigs in them, bottles with snakes in them, bottles that play tunes; they come from every corner of the world, from banana republics and from monasteries, from one-man-and-a-dog outfits and from the enormous booze conglomerates. Heaven knows who drinks them all. Probably more are used for display than for consumption, but these oh-so-often sticky and sickly substances have one fine use. They make great cocktails, either as an additive, as has been in so many of the preceding recipes, or as a main ingredient. Here are a few ideas for cocktails using liqueurs and cordials as a base.

ADAM'S APPLE
Fill tall glass with ice cubes. Add 1½ oz Galliano. Fill with

"*Well, you said I had enough to drink . . . and I had to do something to pass the time!*"

apple juice. Squeeze ¼ section fresh lime into glass. Drop
in lime shell.

ANGEL'S DELIGHT
¼ oz grenadine
¼ oz triple sec
¼ oz creme de yvette
¼ oz fresh cream
*Pour carefully, in order given, into pousse cafe glass, so that
each ingredient floats on preceding one.*

ANGEL'S TIP
¾ oz creme de cacao
¼ oz sweet cream
*Float cream and insert toothpick in cherry and put on top.
Use pousse cafe glass.*

ANGEL'S WING
1/3 oz creme de cacao
1/3 oz brandy
1/3 oz sweet cream
*Pour ingredients carefully, in order given, so that they do
not mix. Use pousse cafe glass.*

APRICOT SOUR
1½ oz apricot flavored brandy
Juice ¼ lemon
Soda
*Shake brandy with lemon and ice; strain into sour glass; add
splash of soda. Garnish with orange slice and cherry.*

CARIBINI

1 oz Galliano
1 oz lime juice
1 oz orange juice
¾ oz creme de noyaux
Shake with ice and strain into cocktail glass.

DUBONNET FIZZ
Juice ½ orange
Juice ¼ lemon
1 teaspoon cherry flavored brandy
2 oz dubonnet
Shake well with cracked ice and strain into 7-oz highball glass. Fill with carbonated water and stir.

DUBONNET HIGHBALL
1 cube of ice
2 oz dubonnet
Fill 8-oz highball glass with ginger ale or carbonated water. Add twist of lemon peel, if desired, and stir.

ETHEL DUFFY
¾ oz apricot flavored brandy
¾ oz creme de menthe (white)
¾ oz curacao
Shake well with cracked ice and strain into 3-oz cocktail glass.

FIFTH AVENUE
1/3 oz creme de cacao
1/3 oz apricot flavored brandy
1/3 oz sweet cream
Pour carefully, in order given, into pousse cafe glass, so

that each ingredient floats on preceding one.

GOLDEN BUNNY
½ oz Galliano
½ oz dry sherry
½ oz Scotch whiskey
White of 1 egg
Juice of 1 lime
Shake with ice and strain into champagne glass.

GOLDEN DREAM
1 oz Galliano
½ oz cointreau
½ oz orange juice
½ oz cream
Shake in cracked ice, strain into cocktail glass.

GRASSHOPPER
¾ oz creme de menthe (green)
¾ oz creme de cacao (white)
¾ oz light sweet cream
Shake well with cracked ice and strain into 3-oz cocktail glass.

GRENADINE RICKEY
1 cube of ice
Juice ½ lime
1½ oz grenadine
Fill 8-oz highball glass with carbonated water and stir. Leave lime in glass.

GALLICE

¾ oz Galliano
¾ oz Grand Marnier
Stir over ice. Serve on the rocks and add orange rind twist.

GOLDEN GLOW
1 oz Galliano
1 oz Drambuie
1 oz gin
Stir with ice. Serve in cocktail glass.

MILANO
1 oz Galliano
1 oz gin
1 oz fresh lime juice
Shake with ice and strain into cocktail glass. Serve with cherry.

MINT HIGHBALL
1 cube of ice
2 oz creme de menthe (green)
Fill 8-oz highball glass with ginger ale or carbonated water. Add twist of lemon peel, if desired, and stir.

PINK SQUIRREL
1 oz creme de almond liqueur
½ oz creme de cacao (white)
½ oz light cream
Shake well with cracked ice and strain into 3-oz cocktail glass.

PORT AND STARBOARD
½ oz grenadine

½ oz creme de menthe (green)
Pour carefully into pousse cafe glass, so that menthe floats on grenadine.

POUSSE CAFE
1/6 grenadine
1/6 yellow chartreuse
1/6 creme de yvette
1/6 creme de menthe (white)
1/6 green chartreuse
1/6 brandy
Pour carefully, in order given, into pousse cafe glass so that each ingredient floats on preceding one.

RAFFAELLO
1 oz Galliano
1 oz Inca Pisco
1 oz white sweet vermouth
1 dash Angostura bitters
1 dash Grand Marnier or triple sec
Shake with ice and serve on the rocks in old-fashioned glass.

STARS AND STRIPES
1/3 grenadine
1/3 heavy sweet cream
1/3 creme de yvette
Pour carefully, in order given, into pousse cafe glass, so that each ingredient floats on preceding one.

VONNIE'S DELIGHT
Fill tall glass with ice cubes. Add 1 oz coffee liqueur. Fill glass ¾ full with milk. Stir. Float ½ oz Galliano on top.

"She's been doing that ever since Harry's party!"

13. WINE COCKTAILS

Cheap domestic wine, particularly in California, is no longer the exclusive preserve of the down-and-out but represents a staple, low-budget beverage for day-to-day consumption for a wide cross-section of society. Some of these very inexpensive wines are quite palatable, others less so. One way to make them more presentable, particularly for parties, is to use them as a basis for a wine cocktail or punch. Here are a few ideas for cocktails based on wine, champagne, port and sherry.

ADONIS COCKTAIL
1 dash orange bitters
¾ oz sweet vermouth
1½ oz dry sherry wine
Stir well with cracked ice and strain into 3-oz cocktail glass.

BLACK VELVET
5 oz stout
5 oz champagne
Pour very carefully into 12-oz glass with cubes of ice and stir very gently.

BROKEN SPUR
¾ oz sweet vermouth
1½ oz port wine
¼ teaspoon curacao
Stir well with cracked ice and strain into 3-oz cocktail glass.

CHABLIS COCKTAIL
2 oz Chablis
½ oz pineapple juice
½ teaspoon maraschino
Dash of orange bitters
Club soda
Mix together with cracked ice and strain into a well-chilled cocktail glass.

BUCKS FIZZ
¼ glass orange juice
Fill with champagne. Use 12-oz Tom Collins glass and stir very gently.

CHAMPAGNE COCKTAIL
Spiral rind of ½ lemon
1 lump sugar
2 dashes bitters
Use 6-oz champagne glass. Fill with champagne.

CHAMPAGNE CUP
Use large glass pitcher
4 teaspoons powdered sugar
6 oz carbonated water
½ oz triple sec
½ oz curacao
2 oz brandy
Fill pitcher with cubes of ice. Add 1 pint of champagne. Stir well and decorate with as many fruits as available and also rind of cucumber inserted on each side of pitcher. Top with small bunch of mint sprigs. Serve in 5-oz claret glass.

HOT SPRINGS COCKTAIL
1½ oz dry white wine
½ oz pineapple juice
½ teaspoon maraschino
1 dash orange bitters
Shake well with cracked ice and strain into 3-oz cocktail glass.

LONDON SPECIAL
Put rind of ½ orange into 6-oz champagne glass. Add:
1 lump sugar
2 dashes bitters
Fill with champagne, well chilled, and stir gently.

MULLED CLARET
Into a metal mug put:
1 lump sugar
Juice ½ lemon
1 dash bitters
1 teaspoon mixed cinnamon and nutmeg

5 oz claret
Heat poker red hot and hold in liquid until boiling and serve.

PORT WINE COCKTAIL
2¼ oz port wine
½ teaspoon brandy
Stir slightly with cracked ice and strain into 3-oz cocktail glass.

PORT WINE FLIP
1 egg
1 teaspoon powdered sugar
1½ oz port wine
2 teaspoons sweet cream (if desired)
Shake well with cracked ice and strain into 5-oz flip glass. Grate a little nutmeg on top.

PORT WINE SANGAREE
Dissolve ½ teaspoon powdered sugar in 1 teaspoon of water.
2 oz port wine
2 cubes of ice
Serve in 8-oz highball glass. Fill balance with soda water. Stir, leaving enough room on which to float a tablespoon of brandy. Sprinkle lightly with nutmeg.

QUEEN CHARLOTTE
2 oz claret wine
1 oz raspberry syrup or grenadine
Pour into 12-oz Tom Collins glass. Add cup of ice; fill with lemon soda and stir.

REFORM COCKTAIL

¾ oz dry vermouth
1½ oz sherry wine
1 dash orange bitters
Stir well with cracked ice and strain into 3-oz cocktail glass.
Serve with a cherry.

SAUTERNE CUP
Use large glass pitcher.
4 teaspoons powdered sugar
6 oz carbonated water
½ oz triple sec
½ oz curacao
2 oz brandy
Fill pitcher with cubes of ice. Add 1 pint of sauterne. Stir
well and decorate with as many fruits as available and also
rind of cucumber inserted on each side of pitcher. Top
with small bunch of mint sprigs. Serve in 5-oz claret glass.

SHERRY TWIST
1 oz sherry wine
1/3 oz brandy
1/3 oz dry vermouth
1/3 oz triple sec
½ teaspoon lemon juice
Shake well with cracked ice and strain into 3-oz cocktail
glass. Top with pinch of cinnamon and twist of orange peel
dropped in glass.

SHERRY COCKTAIL
2½ oz sherry wine
1 dash bitters
Stir well with cracked ice and strain into 3-oz cocktail glass.

Twist of orange peel and drop in glass.

SHERRY FLIP
1 egg
1 teaspoon powdered sugar
1½ oz sherry wine
2 teaspoons sweet cream (if desired)
Shake well with cracked ice and strain into 5-oz flip glass.
Grate a little nutmeg on top.

SHERRY SANGAREE
Dissolve ½ teaspoon powdered sugar in 1 teaspoon of water.
Add:
2 oz sherry wine
2 cubes of ice
Serve in 8-oz highball glass. Fill balance with soda water.
Stir, leaving enough room on which to float a tablespoon of
port wine. Sprinkle lightly with nutmeg.

STRAIGHT LAW
¾ oz gin
1½ oz sherry wine
Stir well with cracked ice and strain into 3-oz cocktail glass.

XERES
1 dash orange bitters
2 oz sherry wine
Stir well with cracked ice and strain into 3-oz cocktail glass.

14. TEQUILA

Tequila, like vodka, has graduated from the its position as a long-forgotten dust-covered bottle on the back shelf. It is now a big seller in cocktail form throughout the United States. It became fashionable initially among the bar hounds of Southern California, exposed to the drink because of their proximity to the Mexican border. Holidays in Acapulco encouraged Americans with adventurous palates to take their first hesitant steps into a new realm of drinking. The traditional lemon quarter and salt technique had a lot of holiday appeal, but stood little chance of establishing a firm foothold in the cocktail lounges of Beverly Hills. No, it all happened with the introduction of the margarita, an eminently drinkable combination of tequila, triple sec and lime. The drink caught on and others were developed until today, tequila cocktails constitute an important part of any self-respecting mixologist's repertoire.

"No, I don't drink myself . . . but I enjoy people who do!"

Tequila is a spirit, generally 80 proof, which is distilled from the agave plant and, far from being a fad, does indeed make an excellent base for elaborate and simple cocktails alike. It has a distinctive yet mellow flavor which is always in evidence, yet seldom overpowering. Unlike vodka and gin, quality and flavor vary considerably from one brand of tequila to another, and it pays to spend a little extra to get one of the better lables even if it is to be used exclusively for cocktails. You really can tell the difference, no matter how heavily camouflaged the spirit becomes.

TEQUILA COCKTAILS

ACAPULCO GOLD
1 oz tequila
2 oz pineapple juice
½ oz undiluted grapefruit juice
1 oz dark rum
1 oz coconut cream (optional)
Shake well with ice cubes and strain into a 12-oz chimney glass filled with fresh ice cubes.

TEQUILA MOCKINGBIRD
2 oz gold tequila
½ lime
2 dashes grenadine
4-6 oz grapefruit juice
Fill an old-fashioned glass three-quarters full with ice cubes; squeeze in lime juice, keeping skin; add tequila and grenadine; top up with grapefruit juice and decorate with lime.

TEQUILA COLLINS

1 oz tequila
1 oz lemon juice
½ oz surgar syrup
½ lime
Club soda
Pour ingredients and juice from lime into a highball glass containing ice cubes; stir well and decorate with lime peel; serve with two straws.

TEQUILA GIMLET
2 oz tequila
1 oz lime juice
Stir with ice cubes in an old-fashioned glass.

TEQUILA SUNRISE
2 oz tequila
½ lime
2 teaspoons grenadine
½ teaspoon creme de cassis
Club soda
Squeeze lime juice into a highball glass filled with ice cubes; drop in lime skin; add remaining ingredients and top up with club soda.

15. BLOWING HOT AND COLD

Sweltering summer days and the biting cold of winter have inspired two entirely separate categories of drinks, designed not only to compensate for the extremes of the weather but also to excite our taste buds and perhaps get us just enough smashed to ignore it. It is a strange but indisputable fact that almost all punches, hot or cold, tend to have a potency quite out of proportion to their taste or actual alcoholic content. Amateurs, beware!

Apart from their almost legendary potential, punches provide a marvelous all-purpose bulk drink for low-budget parties. They can be prepared well in advance and, because there are so many widely varied recipes for them, the punch you serve can be adapted to suit the ingredients most readily available.

Actually, some of the recipes given here are designed to be made up in bulk and served in either a punch bowl or a

"You're still my dream girl, dear. She's merely flesh and blood!"

pitcher, while others are described as single drinks. It is a matter to reduce or increase the volume by multiplying or dividing the quantities of the ingredients proportionately. Once again, it all depends on the size of the party!

PUNCHES FOR A HOT AFTERNOON

APPLE CIDER PUNCH (10 drinks)
2 quarts apple cider
1 pint brandy
Juice of 4 lemons
1 teaspoon cucumber juice
½ sliced cucumber
2 diced apples
Mix together sugar, lemon juice, and cucumber juice, and pour over a large block of ice in pitcher or bowl. Add brandy and cider and chill thoroughly. Put in apple cucumber just before serving in punch cups.

BALAKLABA PUNCH (25 drinks)
2 bottles domestic champagne, dry
2 quarts claret
2 bottles club soda
6 oz maraschino
Juice of 1 lemon
Grated peel of 1 lemon
4 tablespoons sugar
Mix together sugar, lemon peel, lemon juice and maraschino in a bowl or jug; stir; add about twenty ice cubes or single large block of ice together with claret. Add champagne and club soda just before serving.

BARBANCOURT CASSIS PUNCH (10 drinks)

1 cup creme de cassis
1 quart light rum
1 cup dry vermouth
1 bottle champagne

Mix cassis, rum and vermouth in a pitcher and chill thoroughly. Add ice cubes and champagne just before serving in punch cups.

BOMBAY PUNCH (20 drinks)

1 quart brandy
1 quart sherry
¼ pint maraschino
½ pint orange curacao
2 quarts club soda

Combine in a large punch bowl and decorate with fruit as desired. Set bowl in a bed of ice to chill. Just before serving add 4 quarts of chilled champagne.

BRANDY PUNCH (25 drinks)

2 quarts brandy
½ pint curacao
2 oz grenadine
1¼ lb. powdered sugar
Juice of 4 oranges
Juice of 15 lemons

Pour over a large block of ice. Before serving add 2 quarts of club soda.

FISH HOUSE PUNCH (30-40 drinks)

2 quarts dark or medium rum
1 quart brandy

4 oz peach brandy
1 quart lemon juice
2 quarts water
½ pound sugar
Dissolve sugar in water in a large bowl. Stir in remaining ingredients plus a large block of ice; chill for at least an hour and serve in punch cups.

GIN PUNCH (25 drinks)
2 quarts gin
6 oz grenadine
Juice of 20 oranges
Juice of 12 lemons
Pour over a large block of ice and add 2 bottles of club soda. Decorate with fruit as desired.

GOLDFINGER (12 drinks)
2 quarts pineapple juice
8 oz vodka
5 oz Galliano
Stir with ice in pitcher or punch bowl.

GALLIANO SANGRIA
Bottle of full-bodied red wine
4 oz Galliano
Juice of 1 orange
Juice of 1 lemon
Slices of 1 lime, orange and lemon
Mix in pitcher and let stand. When ready to serve, add ice and stir till cold. Add one bottle of club soda (12 oz) and stir gently.

INDEPENDENCE PUNCH
1 fifth brandy
3 fifths claret
1 bottle champagne
Juice of 24 lemons
1 pint strong tea
2 pounds sugar
In a large bowl dissolve sugar in lemon juice; add tea, large block of ice, chilled claret and brandy. Chill and add champagne just before serving.

ORANGE PUNCH (20 drinks)
1 quart vodka
1 quart orange juice
1 quart club soda
1 quart ginger ale
Pour over a large block of ice in a punch bowl; stir, refrigerate and serve in punch cups.

PINEAPPLE PUNCH
1½ quarts moselle wine
5 dashes Angostura bitters
4 oz English gin
1 oz pineapple syrup
1 oz grenadine
1 oz maraschino
Juice of 3 lemons
Mix in punch bowl and add 1 quart club soda. Set bowl in bed of crushed ice and decorate with sliced pineapple.

REGENT PUNCH (15 drinks)
1 pint brandy

1 fifth dry white wine
1 bottle champagne
2 oz curacao
2 oz dark rum
1 pint club soda
½ pound sugar
Juice of 5 lemons

Dissolve sugar in lemon juice; stir in curacao, rum and brandy; add large block of ice; add wine and chill thoroughly. Just before serving, add chilled soda and champagne.

RUM PUNCH

10 quarts white wine
2 pounds brown sugar
2 quarts orange juice
1 quart lemon juice
10 sliced bananas
2 fresh pineapples, cut or chopped
6 quarts light rum
1 quart Jamaica (dark) rum
1 quart creme de banana

Place fruit juice, rinds, bananas, pineapple and wine in a large bowl with the sugar and let stand overnight. In the morning add the rum and creme de banana. Let stand for several hours, then pour over a large block of ice.

THANKSGIVING PUNCH (20 drinks)

1 quart white rum
1 quart cranberry juice
1 quart apple juice
¼ cup lemon juice

Pour over ice cubes in large pitcher; refrigerate, chill and serve decorated with fruit.

INDIVIDUAL COOLERS

ADULT SODA
1 quart club soda
1 quart vanilla ice cream
¾ cup each: Galliano, fresh lemon juice, whipped cream
In 6 tall glasses, blend 2 tablespoons each, Galliano, lemon juice and whipped cream. Then alternate soda and scoops of ice cream. Stir gently. When soda has settled, top with scoop of ice cream. Makes 6 sodas.

APRICOT COOLER
Into 12-oz Tom Collins glass, put:
½ teaspoon powdered sugar
2 oz carbonated water
Stir and fill glass with cracked ice and add:
2 oz apricot flavored brandy
Fill with carbonated water or ginger ale and stir again. Insert spiral of orange or lemon peel (or both) and dangle end over rim of glass.

BOSSA NOVA SPECIAL
1 oz Galliano
1 oz light rum
¼ oz apricot brandy
2 oz pineapple juice
½ oz white of egg
¼ oz lemon juice
Shake well, pour into a tall glass with ice cubes and decorate with fruit.

BRANDY COLLINS
Juice ½ lemon
1 teaspoon powdered sugar
2 oz brandy
Shake well with cracked ice and strain into 12-oz Tom Collins glass. Add several cubes of ice, fill with carbonated water and stir. Decorate with slice of orange, lemon and a cherry. Serve with straws.

BOSTON COOLER
Into 12-oz Tom Collins glass, put:
Juice ½ lemon
1 teaspoon powdered sugar
2 oz carbonated water
Stir. Then fill glass with cracked ice and add:
2 oz rum
Fill with carbonated water or ginger ale and stir again. Insert spiral of orange or lemon peel (or both) and dangle end over rim of glass.

GIN COOLER
Into 12-oz Tom Collins glass, put:
½ teaspoon powdered sugar
2 oz carbonated water, and stir
Fill glass with cracked ice and add:
2 oz gin
Fill with carbonated water or ginger ale and stir again. Insert spiral of orange or lemon peel (or both) and dangle end over rim of glass.

ORANGE GIN COLLINS
Juice ½ lemon

2 oz orange flavored gin
Shake well with cracked ice and strain into 12-oz Tom Collins glass. Add several cubes of ice, fill with carbonated water and stir. Decorate with slice of lemon, orange and a cherry. Serve with straws.

PINEAPPLE COOLER NO. 1
1 oz Galliano
Juice of ½ lemon
Juice of ½ orange
4 oz pineapple juice
Shake with ice, pour into large glass over ice, top with sparkling water.

PINEAPPLE COOLER NO. 2
Into 12-oz Tom Collins glass, put:
2 oz pineapple juice
½ teaspoon powdered sugar
2 oz carbonated water
Stir; fill glass with cracked ice and add:
2 oz dry white wine
Fill with carbonated water and stir again. Insert spiral of orange or lemon peel (or both) and dangle end over rim of glass.

POWERHOUSE
1 oz Galliano
½ oz vodka
½ oz 151 proof rum
1 oz sweet & sour mix
1 oz orange juice
Grenadine to color

Blend or shake with crushed ice. Pour into 12-oz "on the rocks" glass. Add ice cubes.

REMSEN COOLER
Into 12-oz Tom Collins glass, put:
½ teaspoon powdered sugar
2 oz carbonated water
Stir; fill glass with cracked ice and add:
2 oz gin
Fill with carbonated water or ginger ale and stir again. Insert spiral of orange or lemon peel (or both) and dangle end over rim of glass.

RUM COLLINS
Juice 1 lime
1 teaspoon powdered sugar
2 oz rum
Shake well with cracked ice and strain into 12-oz Tom Collins glass. Add several cubes of ice, fill with carbonated water and stir. Decorate with slice of lemon and a cherry and drop lime in glass. Serve with straws.

RUM COOLER
Into 12-oz Tom Collins glass, put:
½ teaspoon powdered sugar
2 oz carbonated water
Stir; fill glass with cracked ice and add:
2 oz rum
Fill with carbonated water or ginger ale and stir again. Insert spiral of orange or lemon peel (or both) and dangle end over rim of glass.

SALT LAKE SPECIAL
¾ oz Galliano
4½ oz grapefruit juice
1½ oz gin
Dash orange bitters
Shake with ice cubes and pour unstrained into 8-oz glass.
Fill with 7Up.

SCOTCH COOLER
2 oz Scotch whiskey
3 dashes creme de menthe (white)
Stir into 8-oz highball glass with ice cubes. Fill with chilled
carbonated water and stir.

SLOE GIN COLLINS
Juice ½ lemon
2 oz sloe gin
Shake well with cracked ice and strain into 12-oz Tom Col-
lins glass. Add several cubes of ice, fill with carbonated
water and stir. Decorate with slice of lemon, orange and a
cherry. Serve with straws.

TOM COLLINS
Juice of ½ lemon
1 teaspoon powdered sugar
2 oz gin
Shake well with cracked ice and strain into 12-oz Tom Col-
lins glass. Add several cubes of ice, fill with carbonated
water and stir. Decorate with slice of lemon, orange and a
cherry. Serve with straws.

WHISKEY COLLINS

Juice of ½ lemon
1 teaspoon powdered sugar
2 oz whiskey
Shake well with cracked ice and strain into 12-oz Tom Collins glass. Add several cubes of ice, fill with carbonated water and stir. Decorate with slice of lemon, orange and a cherry. Serve with straws.

HOT PUNCHES AND HOT COCKTAILS

BRANDY TODDY (Hot)
Put lump of sugar into hot whiskey glass and fill two-thirds with boiling water. Add 2 oz brandy. Stir and decorate with slice of lemon. Grate nutmeg on top.

GALLIANO TODDY
Dissolve 1 teaspoon sugar in tumbler and add 1½ oz Galliano, 1½ oz brandy, 4 dashes of raspberry syrup and fill with boiling water. Garnish with slice of lemon.

GALLIANO & HOT CIDER
Add ½ oz Galliano to mug of hot cider. Garnish with cinnamon stick.

GOLDEN CREAM COFFEE
½ pint (1 cup) heavy cream
¼ cup Galliano
Whip cream to form soft peaks. Stir in Galliano and continue whipping until cream is sufficiently stiff; but do not overwork. Float heaping spoonful in cup of hot black coffee.

GOLDEN CUP

1 quart (4 cups) hot tea
¼ cup sugar
5 cups orange juice
¾ cup Galliano
Cinnamon stick
Fesh mint, orange slices for garnish
Combine all ingredients in saucepan. Simmer five minutes.
Pour into punch bowl and garnish. The punch may be kept
warm on a low flame and reheated as often as necessary.

HOT BRANDY FLIP
1 egg
1 teaspoon powdered sugar
1½ oz brandy
Beat egg, sugar and brandy and pour into Tom & Jerry Mug
and fill with hot milk. Grate numeg on top.

HOT BRICK TODDY
Into hot whiskey glass, put:
1 teaspoon butter
1 teaspoon powdered sugar
3 pinches cinnamon
1 oz hot water
Dissolve thoroughly. Then add:
1½ oz whiskey
Fill with boiling water and stir.

HOT BUTTERED RUM
Put lump of sugar into hot whiskey glass and fill two-thirds
with boiling water. Add square of butter and 2 oz rum. Stir
and grate nutmeg on top.

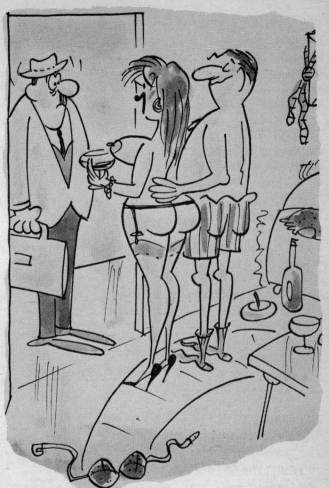

"Come on in, dear. Your friend Harry insisted on throwing a surprise party for you!"

HOT BUTTERED WINE
For each serving—heat ½ cup muscatel wine. Add ¼ cup water just to simmering: do not boil. Preheat mug or cup with boiling water. Pour heated wine mixture into mug and add 1 teaspoon butter and 2 teaspoons maple syrup. Stir well and sprinkle nutmeg on top. Serve at once.

HOT GIN TODDY
Put lump of sugar into hot whiskey glass and fill two-thirds with boiling water. Add 2 oz gin. Stir and decorate with slice of lemon. Grate nutmeg on top.

IRISH COFFEE
Into a pre-warmed 8-oz stemmed glass (or coffee cup), pour 1½ oz Irish whiskey. Add 1 or 2 teaspoons sugar and fill to within ½ inch of top with strong, very hot black coffee. Stir to dissolve sugar. Float to brim with chilled whipped cream. Do not stir. Drink through floating cream.

NIGHT CAP
2 oz rum
1 teaspoon powdered sugar
Add enough warm milk to fill a Tom & Jerry mug and stir. Grate a little nutmeg on top.

RUM TODDY (Hot)
Put lump of sugar into hot whiskey glass and fill two-thirds with boiling water. Add 2 oz rum. Stir and decorate with slice of lemon. Grate nutmeg on top.

ROMAN COFFEE
In a large cup pour 1 oz Galliano, add one teaspoon of

sugar. *Add hot strong black coffee to approximately ½ inch from top of cup, swizzle, then add cream.*

TOM AND JERRY
First prepare batter, using mixing bowl. Separate the yolk and white of 1 egg, beating each separately and thoroughly. Then combine both, adding enough superfine powdered sugar to stiffen. Add to this 1 pinch of baking soda and ¼ oz rum to preserve the batter. Then add a little more sugar to stiffen. To serve, use hot Tom and Jerry mug, using 1 tablespoon of above batter, dissolved in 3 tablespoons hot milk. Add 1½ oz rum. Then fill mug with hot milk within ¼ inch of top of mug and stir gently. Then top with ½ oz brandy and grate a little nutmeg on top.
The secret of a Tom and Jerry is to have a stiff batter and a warm mug.

WHISKEY TODDY (Hot)
Put lump of sugar into hot whiskey glass and fill two-thirds with boiling water. Add 2 oz whiskey. Stir and decorate with slice of lemon. Grate nutmeg on top

"I know you zipped me up before we left the house, dear . . . but this is quite a party!"

16. COCKTAIL HORS D'OEUVRES

Beyond the geniality of the host or hostess and the conviviality and compatibility of the guests, the measure of the ultimate success of a cocktail party generally lies in the quantity of the drinks and the quality of the hors d'oeuvres.

Most people like to nibble while they drink, and with good reason. The proper types of cocktail hors d'oeuvres serve a dual purpose of increasing both the appetite for and capacity for alcohol. The average guest at a cocktail party surely doesn't want to get snockered. To do so would only serve to embarrass his host and himself. The little foodstuffs that are served along with the good drinks are what go to make up the nebulous difference between the success and failure of a well-planned party.

To serve first-class drinks, accompanied only by a basket of pretzels, one of popcorn, some peanuts and a platter of crackers and cheese simply doesn't get the job done. It's rather like wearing your best pair of fine new shoes with no socks. Surely no host dedicated to the effort of serving his guests the best of drinks that would do credit to a high-class restaurant would consider accompanying these first-class spirits with cocktail-hour nibble goodies that more closely resemble the "free lunch" of a waterfront beer bar.

In this specific area we can do well to borrow a page from the books of the professional party-givers. Their approach to the problem seems to be a relatively simple one of maintaining a system of checks and balances between food and beverages by pitting opposites against one another in order to maintain a well-balanced midstream course.

Since the drinks are ice-cold and somewhat bland in flavor, they recommend that these be counterbalanced by the solidity of hors d'oeuvres that are warm to hot in temperature and savory in flavor.

Accompanying the chilled drinks with hot cocktail hors d'oeuvres serves the dual purpose of maintaining the internal temperature of the ingestive and digestive tracts at a normal level and of reactivating the taste buds to combat the chilled alcohol's effects of freezing and anesthetizing of the palate. Each makes the other taste better, and one increases the appetite for the other.

Many very impressive cocktail hors d'oeuvres can be made from small leftover portions of meat, poultry and fish coupled with a few inexpensive and readily obtainable ingredients. The recipes given in this section range from the simplest to some moderately complex gourmet nibbling niceties.

For the host or hostess with limited kitchen facilities and/or experience, here are a few tricky suggestions that will go far toward building your reputation as a home entertàiner.

The frozen foods section of most major supermarkets

feature ready-made cocktail hors d'oeuvres in a wide variety. Most of these are ready to pop right into the oven or broiler and be served. Also there are many old favorites that can be trimmed down to appetizer size. A ready-made pizza pie, frozen and ready to go into oven, can be used plain or "spiked up" with thin slices of pimiento, ripe olives, and bits of meats. After baking, cut it into bite-size pieces (about one-inch squares) and serve on flat trays with cocktail napkins. Frozen eggrolls can also be cut into one-half-inch slices and served on a round tray with toothpicks and a small dip cup of Chinese mustard. Fried fish sticks, cut into one-inch lengths and skewered on a toothpick, can be served with a dip cup of savory red fish sauce. Home fried potato slices (they come frozen and ready to heat in the oven) can be topped with a glob of sour cream and a sprinkling of black lumpfish caviar. Thin-sliced raw turnips make an interesting substitute for potato chips to serve with dips. They also make a crunchy base for a small patty of steak tartare, which is nothing more than lean hamburger meat mixed with egg white and served raw.

Small cocktail hibachis on the bar, each fueled with two charcoal briquettes which allow the guests to cook their own mini-shish kebabs and other skewered goodies, always prove a big hit. These and a couple of fondue pots (Sterno or electric) filled with different cheese melts and *always* served with squares of sourdough bread only, plus perhaps a chafing dish filled with Swedish meatballs (available ready-made from the deli or frozen food department at most supermarkets) or mini-hot dogs will make for a steady supply of hot goodies without tying the host or hostess up in the kitchen. All you'll have to do is occasionally replenish the supply from the reserve stock in the kitchen.

As to how much you'll need in the way of such hors d'oeuvres for a normal length cocktail party, a fairly safe figure for average guests is twenty-five hors d'oeuvres each person. If they're all lumberjacks or football players, or have been on the golf course all day, you may need to increase this somewhat. It isn't as bad as it first sounds. If you have five varieties of bar food, figure five portions of each type per guest. So for twenty guests, you'll need one hundred individual servings of each of the five varieties.

A dip tray with a bland dip surrounded by raw vegetables is extremely popular. They'll look best if you have a corrugated French cutter. Celery, strips of carrot, french fry-sized slices of raw turnip, and similar raw vegetables in season will prove a big hit.

From the broad spectrum of recipes given below you're sure to find a sufficient variety of party "sparker-uppers" that are well within the limits of any budget or level of culinary capability.

FONDUES

Technically, a fondue is anything cooked in hot oil, but the cheese industry of Switzerland has made the world forget the original meaning of the word. To most of us today, a *fondue* is melted cheese in a heated pot into which we dunk and coat hunks of bread.

For the party giver, fondues are a true blessing. They're quick, easy and inexpensive to prepare, require no attention or serving and are considered a gourmet treat by both men and women guests.

Fondues are great "catch-alls" in that you can use left-over bits and pieces of cheeses too small to do anything else with. Mixed together and melted, they assume the status of a culinary creation. Into this you can mix small tidbits of leftover meats, poultry, fowl or seafood. There is a certain alchemy to the fondue pot that magically converts lowly leftovers into lordly treats.

Here are just a few ideas to spark your thinking. This is an area in which you can safely let your imagination run rampant. It is virtually impossible to create a bad fondue.

HOT SHRIMP DIP FONDUE

1 8-ounce package cream cheese
1 10 1/2-ounce can condensed cream of shrimp soup
1 4-ounce jar or tin of cooked peeled shrimp
1/2 cup sour cream
1 teaspoon horseradish sauce
1/4 teaspoon Worcestershire sauce

Heat cream cheese until it becomes soft. Blend in condensed cream of shrimp soup (do not dilute as per package instructions). Add sour cream, cooked shrimp, horseradish and Worcestershire sauce. Stir slowly until well melted and smoothly blended. Pour into fondue pot and place over fondue burner. If desired, this can be made even more impressive-looking by sprinkling surface with chopped parsley, a bit of paprika for color, and floating with tiny deveined cooked bay shrimp.

AVOCADO AND SAUSAGE FONDUE

Break 1/2 pound bulk pork sausage into small bits and cook until tender and slightly browned. Drain off fat and dry sausage bits on paper towels.

In a small saucepan blend 1/2 cup sour cream with 1 cup mashed avocado and 1/3 cup orange juice. Season with 1 teaspoon lemon juice, 1/4 teaspoon salt and a touch of freshly ground black pepper. Stir in the sausage bits and heat until smoothly blended and well melted. Transfer to fondue pot and place over fondue heater. Garnish surface with a sprinkling of paprika, a bit of chopped parsley and a thin slice of lemon, twisted.

TURKEY FONDUE DELIGHT

5 cups cooked turkey white meat, diced into 1/2-inch cubes
1 1/2 cups celery, chopped fine
1/2 cup toasted almonds, chopped
1/4 cup onions, chopped
1/4 cup green pepper, chopped
1/4 cup canned pimiento, chopped
1/4 cup lemon juice
1 1/3 cups Best Foods mayonnaise
1 8-ounce package cream cheese
Blend all ingredients in a saucepan and melt over low heat until smooth and creamy. Transfer to fondue pot and place over fondue heat source. Sprinkle top surface with chopped parsley and paprika. Provide 1-inch cubes sourdough bread and fondue forks for dipping.

FONDUE QUICKIE

Mix two 10 1/2-ounce cans condensed Cheddar cheese soup (do not dilute as directed on can) with one 8-ounce package cream cheese, 1/2 cup dry white wine and several drops Worcestershire sauce in a saucepan. Heat and stir until melted and smoothly blended. Pour into fondue pot and place over fondue heater. Sprinkle top surface with chopped parsley and paprika

In addition to the usual cubes of French or sourdough

bread you can, for variety, provide small stalks of celery, fried fish sticks or cooked shrimp to dip into and coat with the fondue mixture.

SOFT PARMESAN FONDUE (The Bachelor's Delight)
2 8-ounce packages soft cream cheese
1 2 1/2-ounce container shredded Parmesan cheese
1 1/2 cups half-and-half coffee cream
1/2 teaspoon garlic salt
Place all ingredients in electric blender at slow speed until smoothly blended. Heat in saucepan on stove until slightly bubbly. Pour into fondue pot and place on fondue heater. Serve with breadsticks and squares of garlic toast.

SPICED HAM BALLS FONDUE
1/2 pound ground fully-cooked ham (about 1 1/2 cups)
1/2 cup soft bread crumbs
1/4 cup dairy sour cream
2 teaspoons finely chopped onion
1/2 teaspoon prepared horseradish
1 8 3/4-ounce can pineapple tidbits, well-drained and halved

. . .

1 beaten egg
1/2 cup fine dry bread crumbs
Salad oil
Combine ham, soft bread crumbs, sour cream, onion, and horseradish; chill. Shape about 1 teaspoon ham mixture around each pineapple tidbit half. Dip in egg, then in dry bread crumbs. Let stand a few minutes.

Pour salad oil into fondue cooker to no more than 1/2 capacity or to depth of 2 inches. Heat over range to 375 degrees. Add 1 teaspoon salt. Transfer cooker to fondue burner. Have ham balls at room temperature in serving bowl. Spear with fondue fork; fry in hot oil about 2 minutes. Transfer to dinner fork; dip in sauce. Makes about 48 meatballs.

Suggested sauces: horseradish sauce, mustard sauce, spicy pineapple sauce.

MEATBALL FONDUE
Combine 1 beaten egg; 2 tablespoons fine dry bread crumbs; 1 tablespoon finely chopped onion; 2 teaspoons capers, drained; 1/2 teaspoon salt; 1/4 teaspoon dried thyme leaves, crushed; and dash pepper. Add 1/2 pound ground beef; mix well. Form into 3/4-inch meatballs.

Pour salad oil into fondue cooker to no more than 1/2 capacity or to depth of 2 inches. Heat over range to 350 degrees. Add 1 teaspoon salt. Transfer cooker to fondue burner. Have meatballs at room temperature in serving bowl. Spear meatball with fondue fork; fry in hot oil about 1 minute. Transfer to dinner fork; dip in sauce. Makes about 60 meatballs.

Suggested sauces: creamy catsup sauce, spicy tomato sauce, mustard sauce.

DIPPERS' DELIGHTS

Dips are an absolute blessing to the party-giver. They have just about everything going for them. They can be prepared well in advance and served on a moment's notice. Place a small bowl filled with a mixed dip in the center of a large tray or platter, surround with corrugated potato chips, sliced raw vegetables, small celery stalks or carrot spears and you have "instant party."

Fondues are a form of dip, but they are always served

hot. If it's hot, it's a fondue—if it's room temperature or chilled, it's a dip.

Dips have achieved such popularity in recent years that they are now available canned, frozen or dehydrated in nearly as many varieties as soups and salad dressings. As such, they are a tremendous time-saver for the busy host or hostess. You can start with one of these ready-made dip mixes and embellish on it in whatever way your imagination and pantry contents allow.

Here are a sampling of dip recipes, intermixed with a few other hors d'oeuvres that go hand-in-hand with them:

CRANBERRY-PINEAPPLE CHUNKS
Several hours ahead: Press one 1-pound can jellied-cranberry sauce through sieve. Stir in 2 teaspoons vinegar, 1/2 teaspoon prepared mustard. Refrigerate until well chilled. Use as dunk for fresh, canned, or frozen pineapple chunks.

PARTY DIP
1 3-ounce package soft cream cheese
1 tablespoon light cream
1 tablespoon chili sauce
2 teaspoons grated onion
1/4 teaspoon salt
1/8 teaspoon dry mustard
Few drops Worcestershire
Dash pepper
Day before or early in day: In small bowl, thoroughly blend cream cheese, light cream, chili sauce, onion, salt, mustard, Worcestershire, and pepper until smooth and creamy; refrigerate until ready to serve.

At serving time: Pass Party Dip with cucumber fingers,

green-pepper strips, Pascal-celery chunks, red radishes, firm red-tomato wedges, crisp endive leaves. Makes 1/2 cup.

SAGE-CHEESE DIP

1 3-ounce package cream cheese
2 tablespoons milk
1/2 teaspoon leaf sage
Round scalloped crackers

Day before: With back of spoon, rub cream cheese against side of bowl till creamy. Slowly stir in milk and sage; then refrigerate. To serve, arrange in small bowl and surround with crackers. Guests dip crackers into cheese. Makes 3/4 cup.

GREEN-DRAGON DIP

1 ripe avocado
1 3-ounce package soft cream cheese
3 tablespoons mayonnaise
Dash lemon juice or vinegar
1/4 teaspoon seasoned salt
1/8 teaspoon pepper

Early in day: Peel, pit, and mash avocado. Mix with remaining ingredients. Turn into serving bowl. Refrigerate until serving time. Serve on tray, with potato chips for dunking.

INDIAN CURRY DIP

1 pint sour cream
1 pint mayonnaise
2 tablespoons curry powder
2 tablespoons monosodium glutamate
Salt, pepper
Hot pepper sauce, soy sauce

"*Dear, this is Miss Tabney . . . a young lady I've been indiscreet with. Now, be honest . . . do you blame me?*"

Few drops yellow food color
Combine sour cream, mayonnaise, curry powder and mono-sodium glutamate. Add salt, pepper, hot pepper and soy sauces, to taste. Add food color. Blend well and let stand in refrigerator overnight. Makes 1 quart.

WELSH RAREBIT
1 pound Cheddar cheese, grated
1 cup beer
2 tablespoons butter
1/2 teaspoon dry mustard
2 teaspoons Worcestershire sauce
Cayenne pepper
Toast or chips
Combine beer, butter, mustard, Worcestershire sauce and a few grains of cayenne pepper in the top of a chafing dish. Cook over hot, not boiling, water for 5 minutes or until butter melts, stirring constantly. Add grated cheese and cook for 10 minutes or until cheese melts and mixture is thoroughly blended, stirring frequently.

THE GREEN AVALANCHE (Avocado Dip)
2 avocados
1/4 cup mayonnaise
2 tablespoons lemon juice
1 teaspoon chili powder
1 garlic clove, mashed
Freshly ground black pepper
Corn chips
Peel avocados and mash the pulp. Add other ingredients and mix well. Cover and let stand for at least 1 hour. Serve with corn chips. Makes about 2 cups.

SHRIMP REMOULADE

In a bowl place 1 cup mayonnaise with 1 teaspoon prepared mustard and 1 teaspoon each of minced gherkins, capers, parsley and chives. Add 1/2 minced clove of garlic and 1/2 teaspoon anchovy paste. Salt and pepper to taste. Mix thoroughly. This is sufficient sauce for 2 pounds of cooked shrimp. Store in refrigerator. Serve sauce, thoroughly chilled, in a bowl surrounded by ice-cold shrimp on toothpicks.

MIXED HERBS DIP

Flavoring so subtle no one will be sure quite what's in it— and everyone will want to know!

1 8-ounce package cream cheese
6 tablespoons milk or cream
1 teaspoon chicken seasoned stock base.
1 tablespoon hot water
1 tablespoon instant minced onion
1/2 teaspoon Bon Appétit
1/2 teaspoon marjoram leaves
1/2 teaspoon tarragon leaves
1/2 cup finely minced, cooked chicken, shrimp, clams or crab meat

Have cheese at room temperature. Beat until creamy. Gradually stir in milk or cream and seasoned stock base which has been dissolved in hot water. Add remaining ingredients, mixing well. Serve with an assortment of crisp crackers or chips. For an interesting idea use as a filling for marinated mushrooms or bite-size tart shells. Makes about 1 cup.

DILLY WEED DIP

1 cup commercial sour cream
1 teaspoon dill weed

1/8 teaspoon onion powder
1 teaspoon Bon Appétit
Dash monosodium glutamate
Thoroughly mix together all ingredients. Refrigerate at least 1 1/2 hours to blend flavors. Excellent served with crackers, chips or crisp raw vegetables. You will also find this delicious served on hot baked potatoes. Makes 1 cup.

TIDBITS IN BLANKETS
Select any of these tidbits. Wrap in thin strip of bacon. Secure with toothpicks. Broil under moderate heat until bacon is crisp.
Cooked shrimp
Oysters
Stuffed olives
Pickled onions
Watermelon pickle
Sautéed chicken livers

SARDINE DIP
Blend 1/2 pound cream cheese with 3 tablespoons lime juice. Add 2 cans of sardines mashed with their own oil, 3 tablespoons finely cut chives and 1/2 cup chopped parsley. Add salt to taste, then cream to dipping consistency.

KIP-NIPS
Add lemon juice to minced kippered herrings. Spread on squares of bread, roll and fasten with toothpicks. Brush with butter; broil.

CRAB MEAT DIP
1 cup crab meat

1/4 cup lime or lemon juice
1 3-ounce package cream cheese
1/4 cup heavy cream
2 tablespoons mayonnaise
1 teaspoon instant minced onions
1/8 teaspoon garlic powder
1 teaspoon shredded green onions
2 dashes cayenne or red pepper
1 teaspoon Worcestershire sauce
1/2 teaspoon salt
1/8 teaspoon monosodium glutamate

Marinate crab meat in lime or lemon juice 30 minutes. Beat together cream cheese, cream, mayonnaise and seasonings until smooth and creamy. Fold in marinated crab meat. For a really attractive service, serve in a deep shell or shell-shaped bowl nested in crushed ice with an interesting arrangement of bite-size pieces of Chinese cabbage, celery, sliced cauli-flowerettes, green peppers and thin, wide slices of carrot. Do not forget a basket of crackers or chips. Makes about 1 1/2 cups.

HAM RAFTS
Add grated Cheddar cheese and condensed tomato soup to ground boiled ham. Season with horseradish and mustard. Spread on toast squares and heat in broiler until browned.

CHEESE POTATO CHIPS
Sprinkle potato chips with grated cheese. Broil slightly to melt cheese and heat chips. Serve promptly.

AVOCADO HAM SPREAD
Mash half-ripe avocado with canned deviled-ham spread.

Serve with corn chips.

CHEESE BALL WITH SESAME SEEDS
1/4 cup sesame seed
2 tablespoons instant minced onion
1 teaspoon beef flavor base
2 tablespoons lemon juice
1/2 pound medium sharp cheese
2 tablespoons mayonnaise
1 tablespoon ketchup
1 teaspoon Worcestershire sauce
1 teaspoon dry mustard
Toast sesame seed in 350-degree oven 15 minutes or until lightly browned. Soak onion and beef flavor base in lemon juice. Grate cheese. Mix all ingredients, except sesame seed, until well blended. Shape into ball. Spread toasted sesame seed on waxed paper; roll cheese ball in seed until outside is coated. Chill. For a festive party idea serve on a tray with a cheese knife. Surround with assorted crackers and Melba toast. Excellent when spread on toast rounds and broiled until cheese melts. Makes good sandwiches. Makes 1 cup.

ROQUEFORT DIP WITH HERBS
1 8-ounce package cream cheese
1 3-ounce package Roquefort cheese
1 teaspoon beef flavor base
1 tablespoon hot water
1/2 teaspoon dry mustard
1/2 teaspoon herb seasoning
Dash nutmeg or mace
5 tablespoons commercial sour cream or milk
Have cheese at room temperature. Dissolve beef flavor base

in hot water. Combine all ingredients, mixing thoroughly. Serve with crackers, chips, celery or carrot sticks. Makes about 1 1/2 cups.

BLUE CHEESE SPREAD
Place 1/2 pound Bleu cheese in a small mixing bowl. Cover with a mild blended whiskey. Marinate in the refrigerator for 2 hours. Blend cheese thoroughly with 5 tablespoons cream cheese, add 2 stalks of finely chopped celery and blend again. Wrap securely and chill in the refrigerator overnight. To serve place in wooden bowl surrounded by saltine crackers.

HAM BALLS
Combine 6 chopped hard-boiled eggs, 1 tablespoon minced chives or onions, 1/2 cup ground cooked ham, ground pepper, 1/4 cup mayonnaise. Shape into small balls. Roll balls in 2/3 cup chopped walnuts.

CHEESE PUFFS
2 cups grated natural sharp Cheddar cheese
1/2 cup soft butter
1 cup sifted all-purpose flour
1/2 teaspoon salt
1 teaspoon paprika
48 stuffed olives
Blend cheese with butter. Stir in flour, salt, paprika; mix well. Wrap 1 teaspoon of this mixture around each olive, covering it completely. Arrange on a baking sheet or a flat pan, and freeze firm. Then place in two or three small plastic bags, tie, and return to freezer. To serve: Bake 15 minutes at 400 degrees.

TASTY TUNA

1 can chunk-style tuna (1 cup)
1 3-ounce package soft cream cheese
1 tablespoon mayonnaise
1 tablespoon chopped capers
1/2 teaspoon soy sauce
1 teaspoon horseradish
1/4 teaspoon each: garlic, celery, and onion salts
1/4 teaspoon monosodium glutamate
Combine all ingredients. Makes 1 1/2 cups.

ANGOSTURA CHEESE

1 3-ounce package soft cream cheese
2 teaspoons anchovy paste
1 tablespoon chopped stuffed olives
1 teaspoon soft butter or margarine
1/2 teaspoon minced onion
1/4 teaspoon prepared mustard
3/4 teaspoon Angostura bitters
Combine all ingredients. Makes about 1/2 cup.

TANGY EGG

4 minced, hard-cooked eggs
3 crumbled crisp bacon slices (optional)
1 teaspoon horseradish
1 teaspoon minced onion
1 teaspoon Worcestershire
1/4 cup mayonnaise or salad dressing
1/4 teaspoon salt
1/8 teaspoon monosodium glutamate
Combine all ingredients. Makes 1 cup.

HOT CHEESE BALLS

4 ounces soft Camembert cheese
1 3-ounce package soft cream cheese
2 tablespoons soft butter or margarine
1/4 cup all-purpose flour
1/4 teaspoon salt
Dash cayenne pepper
1/4 teaspoon monosodium glutamate
3/4 cup milk
1 egg
2 teaspoons water
Packaged dried bread crumbs

About 2 weeks ahead: Rub cheeses through sieve into sauce-pan. Stir in butter, flour, salt, cayenne, monosodium gluta-mate, milk; blend until smooth. Heat, stirring, until thickened. Pour into shallow plate. Cool; then refrigerate until mixture can be easily handled. Beat egg with water. Form cheese mixture into small balls; roll in dried crumbs; dip into egg mixture; then roll in crumbs again. Fry, 3 or 4 at a time, in deep fat heated to 375 degrees until golden and crisp—about 50 seconds. Drain. Cool; freezer-wrap; freeze. To serve: Unwrap frozen balls; place on baking sheet. Bake at 400 degrees 10 to 12 minutes, or until hot. Makes about 4 dozen.

TUNA PICKUPS

1 tablespoon butter or margarine
1 tablespoon flour
1/3 cup milk
1/4 teaspoon salt
1 teaspoon grated onion
Dash liquid hot pepper seasoning

1 can chunk-style tuna
1/2 cup chopped ripe olives
2 tablespoons diced pimiento
1 package piecrust mix; or your own pastry made with 1 1/2
   cups flour

Early in the day: Melt butter; blend in flour; stir in milk and salt. Cook, stirring, until thick; remove from heat; stir in onion, liquid hot pepper seasoning. Drain oil from tuna. Stir tuna into sauce, also olives and pimiento; cool. Roll pastry very thin; cut into 2 1/2-inch squares. Place rounded teaspoonful of filling in center of each square; bring two opposite corners together over filling; fasten with toothpick. Refrigerate. At serving time: Start heating oven to 450 degrees. Brush pastry with cream. Bake 10 minutes, or till golden. Serve hot. Makes 2 dozen.

BACON, CHEESE, AND CRESS

1 3-ounce package soft cream cheese
2 tablespoons milk
8 crumbled crisp bacon slices
1/4 cup chopped water cress
1/4 teaspoon grated onion

Combine all ingredients. Makes about 1 cup.

MEAT BALLS ON FLAMING CABBAGE

1 large cabbage
2 pounds round steak, ground
1/2 cup dry red wine
1/2 cup chopped onion
2 garlic cloves, minced
2 eggs, lightly beaten
1/2 cup butter

1 teaspoon salt
Freshly ground black pepper
Garlic tomato sauce
First make the meat balls. Combine round steak, wine, onion, garlic, eggs, salt and pepper. Shape into bite-sized balls. Sauté in butter for 10 minutes or until golden brown. Keep meat balls hot. Then turn back the outer leaves of the cabbage. Out of its center scoop a hollow large enough to hold a container of canned heat. To serve, set the cabbage on a tray. Skewer the hot meat balls on large wooden (never plastic!) sandwich picks and stick these picks into the cabbage. Light the canned heat and bring to high temperature. Serve the meatballs with a dip of tomato and garlic sauce. Recipe makes hors d'oeuvres for about 24.

ANCHOVY SPREAD

1/2 cup soft butter or margarine
1 to 2 tablespoons anchovy paste
1 tablespoon minced onion
1/4 cup minced celery
Combine all ingredients. Refrigerate before using. Makes 2/3 cup.

CHEESE LOGS

Finely grind 1 cup of pecans and 1 clove of garlic. Blend with 1-ounce package of cream cheese and 1 tablespoon A-1 sauce. Shape into a roll about 5 inches long and 1 1/2 inches in diameter. Roll in chili powder until evenly coated then wrap in foil and chill until firm. Slice and serve with crisp crackers.

CRAB-STUFFED MUSHROOMS

1 7 1/2-ounce can crabmeat
2 teaspoons freeze-dried chives
1 tablespoon sherry
1 teaspoon Worcestershire sauce
Salt
White pepper
2 tablespoons butter
1 1/2 tablespoons flour
1/2 cup milk
25 large mushroom caps
Paprika

Chop crabmeat and add chives, sherry, worcestershire, 1/4 teaspoon salt and a dash of pepper. Melt butter and stir in flour. Add milk and salt and white pepper to taste. Cook until thickened. Mix with crabmeat. Fill mushroom caps with mixture, sprinkle with paprika and bake at 350 degrees for 10 to 15 minutes. Makes 25 appetizers.

BACON AND CHILI TIDBITS

1 can (20-ounce) pineapple chunks
24 slices bacon
24 large stuffed green olives
1 cup chili sauce

Drain pineapple reserving 1/4 cup syrup. Cut bacon slices in halves; wrap each half-slice of bacon around a chunk of pineapple. Assemble skewer. Blend chili sauce and reserved syrup; brush over skewers. Broil. Use remaining chili sauce as a dunk.

HAM 'N' EGGS

Cut hard-boiled eggs lengthwise in half and remove yolks. Fill whites with finely ground ham, liberally mixed with mayonnaise. Arrange on a platter and serve with crackers. Blend the yolks with mayonnaise, pepper to taste, and spread on crackers.

HOT HOUSE
Mix Limburger cheese with a small amount of butter. Add grated onion and sprinkle liberally with salt. Spread on crackers.

CHIVE BALLS
Mix equal parts of grated Swiss cheese and minced ham. Add one egg yolk, mustard and salt. Roll in minced chives. Form into small balls and serve with toothpicks.

PICKLE ROLL-UPS
Remove crust from sliced bread and spread slices with cream cheese. Roll each slice of bread tightly around a large sweet pickle. Chill thoroughly and slice to serve.

MARINATED ARTICHOKE HEARTS
1 9-ounce package frozen artichoke hearts
2 tablespoons lemon juice
2 tablespoons olive oil
1/4 teaspoon oregano leaves
1/4 teaspoon chervil leaves
1/4 teaspoon tarragon leaves
1/4 teaspoon garlic salt
Cook artichoke hearts following directions on package. Drain and put in small bowl. Combine remaining ingredients and pour over artichoke hearts. Chill at least 2 hours. You will find marinated artichoke hearts excellent served with egg, sea food or tossed green salad. Serves 4.

SALTED SPICED WALNUTS
2 teaspoons ginger
1/2 teaspoon allspice
5 cups water
1 pound walnut halves
4 tablespoons melted butter
1/2 teaspoon garlic salt or Season-All

Add ginger and allspice to water; bring to boil. Drop in walnuts and boil about 3 minutes. Drain well. Spread in a shallow pan and bake in 350-degree oven 15 minutes or until lightly browned. Remove from oven and toss with melted butter and garlic salt or Season-All.

OLIVE CHEESE BITES
1/2 cup butter or margarine, softened
1/2 pound American cheese, finely grated
1 cup flour
1/2 teaspoon salt
1/8 teaspoon cayenne
1 teaspoon paprika
36 small stuffed olives

Cream butter and cheese together. Blend in flour, salt, cayenne and paprika. Mold 1 teaspoon of pastry mixture around each olive, covering completely. Roll between palms into a ball. Arrange without touching on shallow pan and freeze. At serving time, spread out on baking sheet and bake at 400 degrees until golden, about 15 minutes. Serve hot. Makes 3 dozen.

PICKLE CANAPES
Remove the crust from slices of fresh white bread, using a sharp knife to get a clean edge. Mash Roquefort cheese

"Guess who?"

*thinned with cream and color the mixture pink with paprika.
Spread on the bread slices and roll each slice around a large
pickle. Wrap the rolls in waxed paper and chill. When ready
to serve cut into 1/4-inch slices.*

FILLED EDAM CHEESE
*Hollow out an Edam or Gouda cheese. Crumble the removed
part and combine with 2 teaspoons Worcestershire sauce,
1 tablespoon mustard, a few grains of cayenne, 2 tablespoons minced fresh herbs, then refill the cheese shell.
Serve surrounded by crackers.*

SMOKED TURKEY CIGARETTES
*On paper-thin slices of smoked turkey spread seasoned cream
cheese and roll into "cigarettes." Pierce with toothpicks.*

STEAK TARTARE
2 pounds ground beef
2 eggs
1/2 cup capers
1/2 cup minced onion
2 teaspoons salt
Freshly ground black pepper
Pumpernickel bread
*Mix ingredients together. Garnish with additional capers
and serve raw with thinly sliced pumpernickel.*

MOCK LIVER PATE
1 pound liverwurst
1/4 cup brandy
1/2 cup sour cream
1/4 cup grated onion

1 teaspoon prepared mustard
Mash the liverwurst. Add the rest of the ingredients and mix until smooth and well blended. Chill for at least 2 hours.

TWO-IN-ONE SEA SPREAD
1 cup deveined cooked or canned shrimp, drained
1 6 1/2-ounce can tuna, drained
1 cup mayonnaise or salad dressing
1 tablespoon lemon juice
1 tablespoon grated onion
2 teaspoons prepared mustard
1 teaspoon Worcestershire sauce
1/2 teaspoon garlic salt
1/4 teaspoon monosodium glutamate
1/4 teaspoon salt
Several hours ahead: In bowl, with fork, mash shrimp with tuna. Add mayonnaise, lemon juice, onion, mustard, Worcestershire, garlic salt, monosodium glutamate, and salt; blend thoroughly. Refrigerate.

At serving time: In colorful bowl on a tray, heap Two-in-One Sea Spread, with assorted crisp crackers around it and spreaders nearby. Each guest spreads his own. Makes 2 1/4 cups.

WELSH RAREBIT
2 pounds American cheese, diced
1 tablespoon butter
1/2 teaspoon salt
1/2 teaspoon paprika
1 teaspoon dry mustard
Few grains cayenne
1 cup beer

Toast, bread croustades, or crackers
Melt cheese and butter in double boiler, add seasonings, then beer, stirring constantly until smooth. Serve on toast, bread croustades, or crackers. Serves 8.

DRIED BEEF RAREBIT—*Add 1/2 pound shredded dried beef.*

SARDINE RAREBIT—*Arrange cleaned sardines on toast and pour rarebit over them.*

OYSTER, SHRIMP, LOBSTER, CRAB MEAT, OR TUNA RAREBIT—*Omit 1 pound cheese, add 1 cup fish, 1/4 chopped green pepper, and 1 tablespoon chopped onion to the rarebit and cook until thoroughly heated.*

FINNAN HADDIE RAREBIT—*Use 1 cup milk instead of beer, 1 cup grated cheese, and 1 cup flaked, cooked finnan haddie instead of 2 pounds cheese.*

MILK RAREBIT—*Use 1 cup milk instead of beer.*

CHEESE AND TOMATO RAREBIT—*Omit paprika, mustard, and beer. Use 1 pound cheese, 1 cup bread crumbs, and 2 cups strained tomatoes.*

FLUFFY EGG RAREBIT—*Cook 1 minced small onion and 1 minced green pepper in 2 tablespoons butter. Add 2 cups canned tomatoes and 1 cup grated cheese and heat until cheese melts. Add slowly to 2 well-beaten eggs. Cook in double boiler until thickened. Season with salt and cayenne.*

ROYAL RELISH
Prepare a mixture of cream cheese and India relish. Spread on slices of dried beef. Roll and fasten with toothpicks. Chill before serving.

BROILED ANCHOVIES
2 2-ounce cans flat anchovy fillets
3 slices white bread
Minced parsley
Lemon wedges
Trim crusts from bread. Toast bread on one side only in a broiler under low heat. Cut each slice into 6 strips. Put one anchovy fillet on the untoasted side of each strip. Broil under moderate heat for 3 minutes or until hot. Sprinkle with minced parsley and serve with lemon wedges.

PROSCIUTTO AND MELON
1/2 pound prosciutto, thinly sliced
1 honeydew melon
Freshly ground black pepper
Cut melon into wedges or small pieces. Wrap each wedge in prosciutto. Serve with pepper. Crenshaw, cantaloupe, Persian or honeyball melons may be substituted for honeydew. Serve on wooden skewers or heavy sandwich toothpicks.

CAMEMBERT ALMOND BALLS
8 ounces Camembert cheese
1 cup salted almonds, ground
1 cup dry white wine
1/2 cup sweet butter, softened
Toasted crackers
Place whole cheese in bowl, pour wine over it and let stand

at room temperature overnight or for at least 8 hours, turn-ing cheese once or twice. Drain and discard liquid. Press cheese through a coarse sieve or food mill and blend in soft-ened butter. Chill for at least 3 hours. Shape the cheese into about 24 small balls. Roll the balls in ground almonds, and serve them at once with toasted crackers.

DEVIL'S DISH
Spread toast triangles with deviled ham. Add a small amount of lemon juice and Worcestershire sauce. Cover with second toast triangle spread with sharp cheese. Heat in broiler.

17. BUFFET PARTIES: THE FESTIVE BOARD

If your party plans call for feeding your guests more than just cocktail hors d'oeuvres, you must take into consideration table facilities and seating capacity. For a small dinner party for six to eight people, this presents no grave problem. If, however, you plan to have forty, fifty or more guests, it becomes a rather major factor which can exert a very direct effect upon your proper approach to party menu planning.

Few of us today have a baronial banquet table which can comfortably accommodate this number of guests. This means that the only practical answer is a buffet from which the guests may serve themselves and carry their plates to convenient eating places around a cocktail table, from an end table or, quite often, from plates balanced on their laps. Simply carrying a food-laden plate through the heavy traffic of a crowded living room can prove an obstacle course.

"Part German . . . part Irish . . . part rabbit!"

This is especially true after your guests have been drinking steadily for several hours. The danger of spills and dropped plates that can permanently stain carpets, furniture and clothing is considerable, under even the best of conditions. A little defensive planning, in recognition of these dangers, is your best safety insurance against, at best, an expensive cleaning bill.

Unless all of your guests are highly experienced waiters and waitresses, they will probably be inept at carrying a full plate of food across a crowded floor of merrymakers. There are two simple but valuable tips to bear in mind which will make this simpler for your guests and safer for yourself and your furnishings. The first of these is the style of plate to use and the second is the type and consistency of food provided with which to fill the plate.

Under no circumstances should you use large flat (twelve-inch diameter) dinner plates for a buffet. Use smaller saucer-shaped luncheon or salad plates (eight to ten inches in diameter) with slightly raised edges which minimizes the danger of food slipping off in either carrying or lap balancing while eating. Paper plates should be avoided since they invariably lead to disaster by folding and collapsing at the most inopportune times. Few people today have a sufficient number of proper plates in their china closets for such occasions. Plates, glassware, silverware and even napkins can be rented for the occasion from party rental establishments. This is relatively inexpensive and can often save more than the rental fee by avoiding expensive accidents. If you rent plates for such an occasion be sure to specify that you want "buffet plates." They'll know what you mean.

The next consideration should be the type of foods to serve on your buffet table. As an extreme example of what not to do, just consider that if you had just invested a fortune in pure white carpets and upholstered furniture how foolhardy it would be to equip each guest with a large bowl of bright red borscht or Gazpacho to go staggering about carrying unsteadily.

Unfortunately, all too many inexperienced party-givers fail to take the consistency of buffet dishes into consideration. Soupy chili, meats heavily laden with *au jus* or runny gravies, and salads with highly liquid dressings such as oil and vinegar should be avoided. The ideal buffet food should be something of firm consistency that will tend to hold itself in place on the plate. Foods which by nature of their shape can easily roll off the dish or are slippery enough to slide off readily should be avoided. If such items are essential to your menu they should not be placed on the buffet table but should be served to each guest after he is safely settled in the place where he will eat. The same applies to coffee, tea or other beverages.

Careful consideration of these simple "tricks of the trade" in home entertaining can avoid often irreparable damage to your prized furnishings and humiliating embarrassment to your guests.

The "eye appeal" of the buffet is almost as important as the flavor of the foods served upon it. Rather than a cafeteria counter from which your guests may serve themselves, think of it more as you would a birthday cake or Christmas tree to be trimmed with decorations. A colorful cloth is a good starter. This can be enhanced with floral arrangements or simply garlanded with green leaves. Napkins and silver should be neatly arranged, not just lumped together at one end of the table.

Baked casserole dishes are especially well suited to the

buffet party. Many earthenware casserole pans are very decorative and attractive, especially the Italian and Mexican variety. If you have just the plain Pyrex ovenware, there are silver-plated frames into which these can be fitted that gives them a great air of elegance. Or they can be covered with aluminum foil much as you would a plain clay flowerpot brought into the living room.

Chafing dishes with their cheery little flaming Sterno or alcohol burners have a way of making anything served in them take on an appearance of great importance.

Preparing for a buffet spread gives you a good excuse to polish up all of the seldom used silverplate and drag out some of those fancy cheeseboards and wooden bowls you got for presents and never knew what to do with. Such items add to the festive atmosphere that creates the aura of a festive occasion.

Since this type of party violates the principles of the simple and easy-to-host affairs we've devoted most of this book to, we'll give just three representative recips as samples:

CIOPPINO

This impressive-looking party dish is often referred to as the California fisherman's answer to the classic French *bouillabaisse*. It is a mixed seafood stew which makes a quick and easy gourmet concoction of the leftovers of the day's fishing catch.

Cook it ahead of time in regular pots on conventional sources of heat and then serve it, on the table or buffet, in the chafing dish. Refill the chafing dish from the stove as consumed.

1 quart clams or mussels
1 cup white or red wine

1/2 cup olive oil
1 large onion, chopped
2 cloves garlic, chopped
1 green pepper, chopped
1/4 pound dried mushrooms, soaked in water
4 tomatoes, peeled and chopped
4 tablespoons Italian tomato paste
2 cups red wine
Salt & pepper to taste
1 tablespoon dried basil
1 sea or striped bass (about 3 pounds) cut into serving size
   pieces
2 dungeness crabs, broken into pieces or 1 pound crabmeat
1 pound raw shrimp, shelled
3 tablespoons parsley, chopped

Steam clams or mussels in a pot containing one cup wine until they open. Discard any that do not open. Clams or mussels may either be removed from shells or, if you prefer, left in shells for appearance. Strain off the broth and reserve.

Heat olive oil in a large pot and in it cook onion, garlic, peppers and mushrooms for three minutes. Add tomatoes and cook another four minutes. Add strained broth, tomato paste and the red wine. Season with salt and pepper and simmer for another twenty minutes or so. Adjust seasoning to taste.

Add basil and the bass meat. Cook together for around ten minutes. Now, add clams or mussels, crabs (or broken crabmeat) and shrimp. Continue to simmer for about another five minutes or until shrimp are cooked through.

Transfer to chafing dish, sprinkle with parsley and maintain over chafing dish fire on buffet table. May also be sprinkled with paprika for color, if desired.

By Edie Hilton

VEAL CHASSEUR

2 pounds veal cutlets, sliced 1/4-inch thick
1/4 cup butter or margerine
2 shallots, minced or 2 tablespoons minced onions & garlic
   clove
1 pound mushrooms, sliced thin
1/2 cup dry white wine
2 tablespoons parsley, chopped
1 teaspoon salt
Ground black pepper to taste
Brown sauce

Trim fat from veal and cut into one-inch pieces. Saute veal pieces in butter for about ten minutes, or until golden brown. Remove from skillet and keep hot. Place shallots and mushrooms in fat remaining in skillet and saute for five minutes. Add wine and simmer for fifteen minutes or so until the liquid boils away to half the original amount. Stir in brown sauce, parsley, salt and pepper. Return the cooked veal pieces to this mixture and simmer for five minutes longer.

Transfer to chafing dish, cover and retain at temperature by means of chafing dish flame until used. Place on buffet or table. Do not attempt to pass.

CHIPPED BEEF IN MUSHROOM SAUCE

Here's an easy one that looks like a million in a chafing dish. Even the most inexperienced chef can pull this one off.
3/4 pound dried chipped beef
2 cans condensed cream of mushroom soup
1/4 cup butter or margerine
2 cups fresh milk
1 teaspoon Worcestershire sauce
Freshly ground black pepper (coarse)

1/2 cup toasted almonds, sliced
Serve on toast or Holland Rusk

Soak dried chipped beef in two cups hot water for ten minutes. Drain and discard water. Saute beef in butter in chafing dish for five minutes, stirring constantly. Combine soup with milk but do not dilute soup in accord with instructions on can. Stir until well blended and smooth. Stir soup mixture and Worcestershire sauce into beef and season with ground black pepper. Simmer for ten minutes. Sprinkle surface with toasted almond slices. Maintain at serving temperature on buffet or table by means of chafing dish flame. This will serve six when ladled out of chafing dish and poured over toast or rounds of Holland Rusk.

18. TOASTS

The origin of the drinking toast has become hopelessly lost in antiquity. Artifacts from the heyday of the Roman Empire depict drinkers holding their goblets aloft in the attitude of a toast. There are references to toasting throughout literature from the earliest works to the present.

Toasts fall into a number of categories. Notable among these is a form of salute to the nation and its leader. These are generally brief, almost perfunctory. The Romans toasted "Hail Caesar" and the Nazis "Heil Hitler," the Russians drank to the Czar and the British have historically toasted the King or Queen and the Empire.

We toast our heroes for their feats and accomplishments and our friends with the "For He's A Jolly Good Fellow" type of alcoholic salutation.

We drink toasts to our good health, "A Votre Sante," and to our continued good fortune, "May You Live as Long

"Damn it, Mable, why do you always want to go home just when everybody's starting to have a good time?"

as You Want To, and Want To as Long as You Live"—or "Here's Mud in Your Eye" or the theatrical good luck toast, "Break a Leg!"

Before the big football team we drink a toast to Alma Mater and to victory. Later we toast the valiant effort of our team that went down to defeat 60-0.

Diplomats use toasts to both compliment and humiliate the representatives of other nations. At many such affairs the ultimate purpose seems to be downing potent vodka in an endless procession of toasts back and forth until one side, or both, are hopelessly drunk. Those who wish to emerge victorious often drink a glass of olive oil (to coat the stomach and slow down the effects of alcohol being assimilated into the bloodstream and the fumes of fusel oil rising to the brain) before attending such a state function.

Lovers say sweet things to and about each other by means of proposing private or public toasts. The loser shows the ultimate in good sportsmanship by proposing a toast to the winner.

Motion pictures (probably aided and abetted by the glassware industry) did much to promote the popularity of tossing the glasses into an open fireplace to smash against the brick after each toast. The fad caught on for a while, but two recent developments have caused it to fall from the favor. The first is the meteoric rise in the cost of bar glassware (a \$.15 wine glass now costs \$1.80!), and the second is the screening of the fronts of open fireplaces.

The toast is a nice and genteel gesture and, as such, is an integral part of alcoholic etiquette.

Morbid toasts are often proposed to honor the memory of a deceased drinking companion who has preceded us to "that big tavern in the sky."

Sharp salesmen often use a toast as a sort of a "closer" to their sales pitch. After working a prospect over pretty heavily on a big deal, the salesman will take him to lunch or dinner or perhaps just a few belts after work. At the proper moment he will raise his refilled glass and announce:

"I toast your company loyalty and sound judgment in having reached the decision to award the big new contract to the firm I represent."

This sales trick is known as the "totally assumptive close" because you are not asking for a decision but assuming that it has already been made in your favor. Later the poor slob either will feel obligated, since he already drunk to it, or he may actually be wet-brain-washed into believing that he had indeed already reached the implanted decision.

The mental mechanism of the toast often serves as a very effective device for the practical utilization of the forces of applied psychology. Here are a couple of basic examples of how the really sharp operators use it to improve their barroom and cocktail party pick-up technique:

Romeo has been liberally oiling his new-found Juliet with her favorite drink. When he senses that the "Moment of Truth" is at hand he switches her to a champagne cocktail. He toasts the good fortune of their chance encounter and adds:

"If you like this brand of champagne as much as I think you will, I'll stop by a liquor store and pick us up a magnum of it on our way to the motel!"

Another saloon smoothie uses an even briefer version of the approach of the seductive toast:

"To you!" he proclaims as he locks arms and eyes with her and raises his glass in flattering appreciation.

If she replies to his compliment by replying: "To us!"

he chug-a-lugs the drink and suggests that they leave together immediately before superior competition shows up on the scene.

One fellatio freak has his own unique version of the sex toast. When he encounters a likely-looking chick he orders two glasses of champagne. (Nothing is more flattering to a female than to have a toast drunk to her beauty in champagne.)

"Sante!" he toasts, then adds, "You French?"

If she replies, "I am," he drops her like a hot potato. If she replies, "I do," he escorts her to his pad immediately.

Humorous toasts are perhaps among the most popular and commonly encountered. Some of these follow the general theme of the limerick while others are little more than brief anecdotes, one-line gags or just the punch line from a classic old joke. In this area you can let your imagination run rampant, often creating a timely toast based upon some current event or a recent news item.

Here are a few varied forms which may serve to spark your imagination:

"Here's to the girl who lives on the hill.
    She won't, but her sister will.
Screw her . . . here's to her sister!"

"How can I tell you of my love for you,
    When I can hardly breathe down here!"

"He who loves not women,
    Wine and song,
Remains a fool,
    His whole life long."

"Welcome to my happy darkness!"

"Let schoolmasters puzzle their brain,
    With grammar and science and learning,
Good liquor, I stoutly maintain,
    Gives genius a better discerning."

"May those bores who think they know it all,
    Come to realize what a pain in the ass they are,
To those of us that do."

"To the booze that fires us and inspires us,
    What else on earth is quite so desirous?"

"To that sly Casanova named Fred,
    Who did everything to get her to bed.
He plied her with booze,
    Removed both her shoes,
Then passed out on the carpet instead."

"T'wixt booze and cooze, t'is hard to choose.
    So let's drink to the cooze,
Least, till we kill all the booze."

"To the girls who believe in the Hereafter,
    At least they know what we're here after!"

"To the broads that we meet in the Fall,
    Who steadfastly refuse to ball,
But then in the Spring,
    They go into their 'thing'
Till we can't hardly keep up at all!"

By Edie Hilton

"To the Spanish ambassador's daughter,
    Who thought she could walk on water,
Till we got caught in the rain, in her castle in Spain,
    Where we came and we came and we came."

"To our wives and mistresses,
    And the fervent prayer that they never meet."

"To my dear wife and the twenty-five years of bliss,
    We were privileged to enjoy before we met!"

"To the valiant Vikings of yore . . .
    Who always had . . . just one more!"

"A toast to the difference between war and peace.
    There never was a good war . . .
May we never have a bad piece!"

"Any time I hear you yell 'Bottoms Up!' I want to
hear nothing more than the clink of glasses!"

19. SO SHALL YE REAP: HANGOVERS

Every language has a word, or more commonly, a phrase for it. To the Germans it's *the wailing cats;* a Frenchman has a *mouth of wood;* Norwegians have *carpenters in the head,* and we have *mouths like the inside of a Japanese wrestler's jockstrap,* or *eyes like pee-holes in the snow.* The only satisfactory cure for a real out-and-out, god-awful hangover is a humane killer. Every bar, public or private, should carry one as a matter of principle if not as a matter of course. A bolt through the brain would indeed be a merciful release.

In the meantime, since euthanasia and suicide are still frowned upon by the authorities, several less drastic and less satisfactory remedies have been developed as relief from this dreadful illness. The most basic of these is completely effective, but alas merely delays the confrontation to the next day. W.C. Fields was an advocate of Method

One: "Fill a tall glass and drink until dizzy" was his answer. Some of us, however, are forced to face small practical problems, like earning a living, and a state of permanent and complete drunkenness does not go hand in hand with that particular pursuit. What for us lesser mortals?

Everyone has his or her favorite remedy (it is wise to remember in these days of sexual emancipation that hangovers are not exclusively a male malady). Here are a few of them; take your pick; try them out; if they don't make you sick they may cure you. [*Editor's Note:* This paragraph has been kept as short as possible in deference to your eyeballs.]

CHAMPAGNE
A glass early in the morning.

THE SNEAKY PETE
Champagne with a Cognac float. Simply pour a half-filled glass of chilled champagne, then add a float of Cognac, poured over a bottoms-up spoon.

THE PRAIRIE OYSTER
1 egg
1 teaspoon Worcestershire sauce
1 teaspoon catsup
1/2 teaspoon vinegar
Pinch of pepper
Tabasco sauce
Put the whole egg into a 5-ounce Delmonico glass; add the other ingredients. Gulp down.

1/2 teaspoon lemon juice
1/4 teaspoon Worcestershire sauce

3 dashes salt
3 dashes pepper
2 1/2 ounces vodka
4 ounces tomato juice
2 ounces beef bouillon

1 teaspoon sugar
1 1/2 ounces vodka
Pour in a Tom Collins glass and fill with milk.

2 ounces Cognac
2 ounces rum
4 ounces milk
4 ounces cream
2 teaspoons sugar
Shake with ice and strain.

1/2 ounce tequila
1 bottle cold beer
Mix and drink quickly.

1 ounce vodka
1 ounce tomato juice
1/2 ounce clam juice
Dash of Worcestershire sauce
Dash of salt
Juice of one lime
Lemon twist

3 tablespoons ketchup
1 egg yolk
Dash of Worcestershire sauce

1/2 ounce brandy
Blend, add ice, and sprinkle with paprika.

1/2 ounce tequila
4 ounces orange juice
2 ounces tomato juice
1 ounce lemon juice
10 drops Tabasco sauce
Salt and pepper to taste
3 drops grenadine
2 drops Perry sauce

1 ounce vodka
3 ounces clam juice
Dash of Tabasco sauce
Juice of one lime
Pour into highball glass and fill with ice cubes.

If you have tried all the above with no success, then perhaps you're ready for solids. Food, if you can keep it down, is a sure fire remedy for many people. Many favor very spicy dishes; a bowl of hot chili for instance. Here are a couple of specially designed breakfast for hangover sufferers. They were invented by the proprietors of two well-known European hostelries.

ROSIE'S SWISS BREAKFAST CHEESE SALAD
1 thick slice Emmantaler cheese
2 tablespoons French olive oil
2 tablespoons white wine vinegar
1/4 teaspoon German mustard
1/4 teaspoon salt

Freshly ground pepper
Stir the oil, vinegar, and seasonings in a deep soup plate. Scatter in the cheese, cut into 1/2-inch cubes, and toss with a wooden fork and spoon until each tiny cell of the Swiss has been washed, oiled, and polished with the soothing mixture.

  Drink the juice, too, when you've finished.

DRUNKS' SOUP

For 1 large hangover:
1 cup sauerkraut juice
1 cup water
1 cup cabbage, cut up fine
2 frankfurters
3 shallots
2 tablespoons butter
2 tablespoons flour
1/2 teaspoon salt
1/2 teaspoon paprika
Put the water and sauerkraut juice into a saucepan. Add the shredded cabbage and the frankfurters cut into thin slices. Cover the pan and cook for 1 1/2 hours.

  Saute the shallots in the butter until they are soft but not brown. Stir in the flour, salt, and paprika, then gradually add the soup mixture, stirring all the while. When all the soup has been thickened, bring it to a boil and serve. If your hangover hasn't vanished during the cooking, it will during the eating.

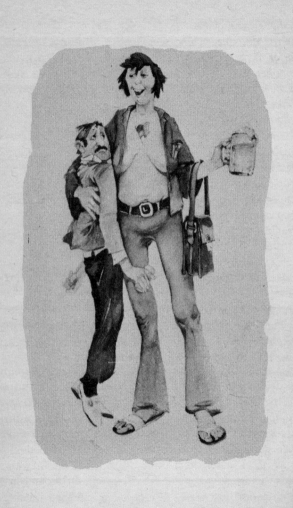

20. FUN AND GAMES

Outstanding hosts and hostesses whose parties are always considered memorable events have often gained their enviable reputations simply by recognizing that giving a successful party involves more than satiating the guests' appetites for food and drink.

The primary purpose of giving a party is to *entertain* your guests. This involves something more than simply genteel and polite hospitality. We have all had the sad and unfortunate experience of attending a party where it was obvious that the host or hostess had gone to a great deal of effort and expense. The drinks were excellent and the cuisine super, but some mysterious secret ingredient was missing. A certain spark never quite came off to ignite the fireworks display of friendly conviviality. Everyone sat around in a big circle and just stared at each other and their watches. After a while nobody spoke until they were spoken to and the whole affair took on the atmosphere of one of those Sunday afternoon "duty sessions" in Aunt Martha's parlor when we were kids, all dressed up and squirming to get the hell outta there.

If we accept the view that a party is a form of home entertainment, we should take care to relate it more closely to big screen television than 8-mm home movies. After all, entertainment is a facet of show business. It would be a sad commentary on our sincere efforts to throw a successful and fun type party to have our guest, safely back at home, remark: "For this, I missed Columbo!"

This does not mean that you should hire a troupe of professional entertainers to put on a poor man's Las Vegas floor show. Nor does it mean that you should put on a piano or violin recital at which your guests are a captive audience. It simply means that you should devote a bit of thought to trying to get a little guest participation in fun and games going. Of course, if you're entertaining the fellow members of your neighborhood swingers' group, the fun and games will take care of themselves in due course. If it isn't that kind of a get-together, a little planning and effort on your part will pay party dividends.

The type of tricks and little games you'll want to get started will, of course, depend largely upon the type of guests you'll be entertaining and their particular interests and forms of activity.

Bottle Cap Dexterity:

The "crown" caps that you snap off of the bottles of mix you'll be using anyway can provide a lot of fun and laughs at the bar.

Place one bottle cap, bottom down, on a paper napkin,

and bet friends at the bar that they can't turn it over using just one finger on the top of it. Some mechanically minded drinkers will reason that the trick is to establish a vacuum between the bottle cap and their fingertip. They'll be able to lift it off the napkin this way, but getting it off the fingertip and getting the finger out of the way so that it falls top side down back onto the napkin, without the help of another finger, is almost impossible. Some will moisten the fingertip, others will dry it. They'll treat the cap like a tiddlywink and try to flip it over. The greater the pressure they apply to one edge the more it will dig into the paper napkin and defy reversal.

Then show them how easy it is, but tell them you'll demonstrate how to do it only once. After that, they'll have to turn it over the way you did before they get another drink. The harder and longer they try (barring a miraculous bit of luck!), the more impossible it becomes. The trick is in the light touch. Dry your fingertip (the middle finger usually works best) and just slightly graze the upper edge of the crown cap in a 45-degree downward movement. It may take a couple of tries, but it will flip over almost magically. Naturally, you'll practice and rehearse this to get it down pat before pulling it on your guests.

The three-bottle cap turnover is another fun-with-fingers bar trick that will produce instant frustration for most who try it. Arrange three bottle caps, top down, with the crinkled edge openings facing upward, touching each other in a cloverleaf pattern on a paper napkin. Explain that this is a very simple little trick which any child can master in a minute. All you want them to do is to place the thumb, index finger and middle finger together in a triangle. Place them into the three open bottle caps, squeeze, and pick them up, then turn them over. Demonstrate the pickup part only, bringing your hand straight down into the caps. Anyone can pick up the three in this manner with no difficulty. Make sure they see your hand going straight down into the caps. Now look up and get their eyes. While their attention is diverted flatten your hand and approach the bottle caps again in as flat an attitude as possible. Put your index and center finger into the two farthest away from you. Instead of putting your thumb into the third one, closest to you, place it on the outside edge and press lightly inward. The three will hang together due to the meshing of their corrugated edges. Now with your hand flat simply turn them over and slide your flattened hand out, laying them slowly down onto the napkin in the reversed position. Announce that it's just as simple as that and invite them to do it. They'll pick them up in the straight-down approach that you demonstrated. When they turn them over, they are several inches above the napkin, and they can't get their hand out of the way. They'll try to drop them and jerk their hand out of the way. Almost invariably at least one cap will land the wrong side up.

Here again, this is a little trick of dexterity that relies upon the angle of approach. Practice it a few times beforehand until you get it down pat. Its utter simplicity is what makes it so frustrating.

The Self-Hypnosis Trick:

The patter which precedes this trick tells of how, on a trip to India, you watched in fascination as the Indian fakirs walked barefoot over beds of live hot coals. The coals are actually hot, since papers and cloth thrown onto them by members of the audience burst into instant flame, and yet the mystic ones seemed to feel no pain and the tender skin of their feet was not burned by the slow walk across the long red-hot runway. After much persuasion and "palm-greasing" you were able to learn the secret of how this physically impossible feat was accomplished. It is simply an application of powerful forces of self-hypnosis by means of which the brain tells the body what will hurt it and what won't. In this case the brain convinces the feet that they are incapable of feeling or being burned by intense heat. Conclude by saying that after considerable exercise of mental discipline you succeeded in mastering the trick yourself.

At this point someone is sure to ask you to prove it by giving a demonstration. You should decline, and appear to be trying to back down from your statement. Then finally appear reluctantly to give in to their pressure. Tell them that you have no intention of setting fire to your carpets to prove that you can mentally will yourself immune to pain. Ask someone in the crowd who is smoking if the lit end of their cigarette is hot. Have him flick the ash and take the cigarette, displaying the glowing red tip. Wipe your hand to show that your fingers aren't wet. Then hold the cigarette between thumb and forefinger with the glowing tip firmly planted against your bare fingertip. Turn your hand over and then move the glowing tip over to the next (middle) finger and finally reverse it and press the lit end against your thumb. As a finale to this little demonstration rub the lit end between your thumb and fingers to snuff it out completely. Wipe the ashes from your fingers and ask if anyone else has faith enough to try it.

Here's how it's done: Before you start your little spiel, surreptitiously remove an ice cube from your drink. Press your thumb, index and middle finger tightly to its surface with your hand out of sight as you go into your patter about the fakir. Be sure to hold it long enough (two minutes or so) that your fingertips will become numb and frozen. Drop the remains of the ice cube to the floor, dry your hand on your pants and then take the cigarette and hold it. Each fingertip will be immune to the heat or any burning effect for at least fifteen seconds.

ESP Games:

Everyone seems to have a curious interest in Extrasensory Perception. Steer the conversation to this subject and then suggest an experiment or two.

Give someone a deck of cards and ask them to select, but not display, five cards as different as they can find them. Explain by this that you mean no more than two of any one suit. Also you don't want all picture cards, and the number cards should be as different and widespread as possible. Ideally you'd like to come up with one ace, perhaps a king and a jack of opposite colors, and maybe a seven and a two of opposite colors.

Select a *subject* of the opposite sex to assist you in the experiment. Explain to this person and to the others that this is *not* a card trick, but an experiment in a metaphysical phenomenon, and therefor it may not work. The five cards which someone has selected are in a little pile, face down, in front of you. Tell the subject that in a minute or so you will ask them to close eyes and hold left hands with you. Their right hand should be poised above and near the cards which you will hold outstretched to them. Now take the cards and, without letting the subject see them, spread them out in as wide a fan as possible. Explain that you are fanning them widely to avoid or lessen the danger of the

subject taking two cards at once. Tell them that they are to give no consideration to where the card which will be named to them is located. Rather they are simply to visualize that card and burn its appearance into their mind. You will tell them when to reach out and select it with their eyes still closed. The idea is for them to allow *your* mind to guide *their* hand. It simply won't work if they try to fight you or to second-guess you. They must have faith in your ability mentally to guide their hand to the selected card.

Of course, point out that you cannot simply move the cards around until the one selected is beneath their grasping fingers, since all of the others, whose eyes are wide open', will be watching you.

Now hold the cards out toward the subject and clasp left hands with them. Tell them to hold their other (right) hand aloft and to remember where the cards are but to make no move toward them until told to do so. Again tell them only to visualize the card but not its location among the five. Then have your subject close their eyes. Now ask someone else in the group to select a card and name it aloud but not to point to it.

Repeat to the subject, who will have heard the spoken selection, "The card which has been selected for you is the King of Spades. You know what a King of Spades looks like. It's a picture card with a double-headed King. It's a black suit and the symbol for spades is pointed at the tops. In the upper corner of the card is a symbol. It is a black K and the spade mark is beneath it. Can you visualize it? I want you to burn that picture into your mind until it's the only thing you can see. You can see nothing now but the image of that King of Spades. Again, I tell you not to consider where it may be. It's my job to guide your hand to it. You can see it very clearly now. That's it. You're doing fine. Now, reach out and take the King of Spades." Say it as a slightly sharp command. "You can see it . . . take it!"

Meanwhile you are giving the silent mental commands: "It's right there. Right where I'm guiding you. Take it, you know which one it is."

The subject will reach out and, if they are being relaxed and cooperative, will almost invariably select the card you have told them to take. You have been staring intently at the card and giving them a series of silent commands to guide their hand. Believe it or not, this will work in over eighty percent of cases, without any type of mechanical trickery. If it doesn't work, don't repeat it with the same subject, but use new cards and a new subject.

Usually, after seeing this ESP demonstration, guests will ask for more. One in which they can all participate will prove most popular. Here's a fun one:

You'll need a volunteer subject, preferably female. Have her leave the room while the other guests pick out an object and place it, either hidden or in plain sight, but they must all know *what* it is, and *where* it is. When the selection is made the subject can be brought back into the room. Explain that her friends have selected an object in the room and will try to guide her to it with their thoughts. Once this is done, have her close her eyes. Turn her around several times, first in one direction and then the other, until she becomes disoriented and doesn't know in which direction she is facing. She must still have her eyes tightly closed.

Tell her to stand very still and erect, eyes closed, mind at rest. The other guests will all concentrate as hard as they possibly can on the object selected and its location. Here, as in the card experiment, she should make no effort to second-guess them and should not try to "think" on her own, but merely listen for the projected messages from others. Tell her to remain very still as everyone concentrates. Soon she will feel a *pull*, as though she were about to fall in a certain direction. When she feels this pulling and falling sensation, she should face in that direction, open her eyes and walk, without hesitation to the object and pick it up and display it to the others whose thoughts have guided her to it.

If everyone cooperates, this tricky looking demonstration will work over eighty percent of the time.

Mr. Wizard—the Real "Mind Blower"!

Bring out a deck of cards and ask if anyone knows any card tricks. Usually, in almost any crowd, somebody knows one or two, which will make a little warm-up to the unbelievable feat you're setting them up for.

Explain that the trick you are about to try is absolutely impossible but, if they'll be patient with you, you'll try it anyway. You will not even touch the cards. Ask someone to shuffle the deck several times and then fan it out and allow a second person to select a card and display it to all. You will then phone someone who is not even present, and that person will name the card which has been chosen. You will say nothing to the person on the other end of the line that can be interpreted as a signal or tip.

Naturally, they'll all agree that it is impossible. When the card is chosen and placed face up near the phone, you dial a number and wait for the callee to answer. When he does, you say: "May I speak to Mr. Wizard, please. Very well, I'll hold on." After a few seconds you say: "Mr. Wizard, will you please tell my guest which card he chose." Then, without further conversation, you hand the phone to the person who selected the card. The voice on the other end of the line says: "The card you chose was the nine of clubs," and then hangs up. Invariably, the answer will correctly name the chosen card. Everyone will want to try it, but say that Mr. Wizard is a very busy man and you don't dare disturb him more than three times.

Here's how it's done: Obviously, you need a confederate who agrees to be at home and available for your three calls at a given time. Since he'll be expecting your call, he'll pick up the phone on the first ring. When he does, he will slowly name suits: "Hearts, Clubs, Spades, Diamonds." When he comes to the suit of the card selected you interrupt, as though the phone has just been answered, and say, "May I speak to Mr. Wizard, please." Now he starts with, "Ace, king, queen, jack, ten . . ." and so on down the deck. When he comes to the proper face card or number, you again interrupt by saying, "Mr. Wizard, will you please tell my guest which card he chose." You hand the phone to the guest and Mr. Wizard names his card and hangs up.

The trick is so utterly simple that people will blow their minds trying to figure it out and always fail.

The Taste Buds Trick:

This is especially appropriate when someone talks about how they can't be fooled and can instantly tell the difference between one brand of vodka or whiskey and another. Ask them if they'll show others their educated taste buds by taking the blindfold test.

They will, of course, expect you to put three different brands or types of liquor before them. Instead, fill three shot glasses, one with Coke, one with ginger ale and the

"Im sorry, Mr. Pilsey . . . I prefer a dirty young man."

third with 7Up. Ask them to identify which is which of each of the three while blindfolded. Believe it or not, not one person in twenty can tell the difference between these three sweet popular mixes while blindfolded!

Party Magic:

There's still enough of the kid in most of us that we get a big kick out of magic tricks. They can spark up a party and tide it safely over the crucial dull period or sinking spell that nearly every party, no matter how well planned, goes through.

If you intend to do any considerable amount of home entertaining of different groups of guests and are stocking your bar and pantry in preparation for such gatherings, it might be a good idea to lay in a little stock of party gimmicks in the form of amusing tricks. These prove especially popular with a group of guests gathered around a home bar.

Local magic and trick shops stock a large variety of highly mechanized illusions which would do credit to the most dexterous sleight-of-hand artist. There are many mechanical decks of cards with which one or more special tricks can be done with a little practice and imagination that appear to require the advanced skill of a master prestidigitator. These are generally quite inexpensive and prove an excellent investment in allowing you, as host, to display a near legendary legerdemain that will amuse and astound your guests.

One such mechanical deck is called "The Svengali Deck." It is what professional magicians call a "strip deck" in that every other card is slightly shorter than the ones between them. If you flip through the deck from front to back, each card will be different, making it appear to be a normal deck of playing cards. Flipped through in the opposite direction, each card becomes the same. This allows a number of mind-boggling tricks that, with a properly developed running patter, can appear complex to the point of being impossible.

Here's one that's always a hit. Remove the cards from behind the bar and flip through them so that each card appears different and normal. Now, placing them face down on the bar, flip through slowly until someone says "Stop," then ask him to take the face-down card that is exposed and show it to everyone but you. Hold the top card you've lifted off the pile so that everyone can see that it is different from the one selected. When all have seen it, have them replace the card face down and you put the others you've been holding on top of it. Now hold the deck of cards facing them with your left hand. With your right run through them slowly so that each card appears for a moment or so. Ask the person who chose the card to tell you to stop when they see the card they selected. When you come to the last card they will say that the one they chose was not in the deck.

"Of course not," you tell them. "I removed it even while you were watching me closely. If you'll look under the clock on the mantel I believe you'll find the card you chose." They will and, of course, it will be their card. Have them replace the card in the deck, then put it away.

Here's how it's done: Since every other card in the deck is the same, no matter where they tell you to stop they'll pick the same card. Before the party you have merely removed one of these identical alternate cards and secreted it under the clock.

Never repeat a trick, but go on to something else.

Magic shops also feature a number of bar drawer gimmicks that are lots of fun. One mind-boggler is a simple nut and bolt. You will have no difficulty running the nut up and down the threads of the bolt, but when anyone else tries this simple movement it will be as if the two had suddenly become welded together into an immobile unit. After they all fail, you screw it up and down effortlessly. Many master mechanics and graduate engineers have gone absolutely bananas trying to fathom this one.

Some of these suggestions may impress you as corny, but with heavy party-giving experience you'll learn that most cocktail party guests tend to get pretty corny themselves and, after a few drinks, are utterly enthralled by them.

ABOUT THE AUTHOR

EDIE HILTON has been called the latter day Elsa Maxwell of party-giving by *The Los Angeles Times, Los Angeles* magazine and *The Hollywood Reporter.*

As a Party Consultant she has been in charge of planning some of the most fabulous parties of recent years amid the glamor and glitter of Bel Air, Beverly Hills, Hollywood and Universal City. Her studio preview parties have served to kick off many of the major motion picture and television productions of the past ten years. In the latter field she serves as Entertainment Consultant to both CBS and NBC. George Christie, author of *The Good Life* and Party Editor of *The Hollywood Reporter,* says: "Party planning by Edie is the surest route I know of to social success in the screen society."

As Southern California's leading gourmet cateress, Edie Hilton is highly experienced at executing, as well as planning, both studio and home parties for the leading producers, directors and stars of the entertainment industry. The same success secrets she shares with her star-studded client list are, for the first time anywhere made available to you in this book. Her Drink Directors have provided many of the trade secrets gleaned from many years experience as professional party givers.

Ms. Hilton provides recipes for hors d'oeuvres, snacks, party buffet and main dishes that are the party favorites of the stars and her other famous clients with their socially sophisticated palates. She studied cuisine and culinary arts under Cordon Bleu, l'Ecole des Trois Gourmandes (Julia Child), and later Michael Field and Dione Lucas. She is the author of several major cookbooks including the current best-seller *The Quiche Cook Book*. She is currently considering carrying on the continuing series of cookbooks of the late radio chef, Mike Roy.

The neophyte or amateur party giver or home entertainer could not have a better team of professional advisors than we have assembled to guide him during the preparation of this book.

The Editors